CONGRESSIONAL POLICIES, PRACTICES AND PROCEDURES

APPOINTMENT PROCESS FOR U.S. CIRCUIT AND DISTRICT COURT NOMINATIONS

OVERVIEW AND ACTIVITY DURING OBAMA'S ADMINISTRATION

CONGRESSIONAL POLICIES, PRACTICES AND PROCEDURES

Additional books in this series can be found on Nova's website under the Series tab.

Additional e-books in this series can be found on Nova's website under the eBooks tab.

CONGRESSIONAL POLICIES, PRACTICES AND PROCEDURES

APPOINTMENT PROCESS FOR U.S. CIRCUIT AND DISTRICT COURT NOMINATIONS

OVERVIEW AND ACTIVITY DURING OBAMA'S ADMINISTRATION

CALEB BOWMAN
EDITOR

NOVINKA
New York

Library of Congress Cataloging-in-Publication Data

ISBN: 978-1-63485-587-7

Published by Nova Science Publishers, Inc. † New York

CONTENTS

PREFACE

The selection and confirmation process for U.S. circuit and district court judges is of continuing interest to Congress. Recent Senate debates over judicial nominations have focused on issues such as the relative degree of success of President Barack Obama's nominees in gaining Senate confirmation compared with other recent Presidents, as well as the time from nomination to confirmation for nominees, and the relative prevalence of vacant judgeships compared to years past. This book addresses these issues, and others, by providing a statistical analysis of nominations to U.S. circuit and district court judgeships during the first six years of President Obama's time in office and that of his three most recent two-term predecessors, Presidents Reagan, Clinton and G.W. Bush.

In: Appointment Process for U.S. Circuit ISBN: 978-1-63485-587-7
Editor: Caleb Bowman

Chapter 1

THE APPOINTMENT PROCESS FOR U.S. CIRCUIT AND DISTRICT COURT NOMINATIONS: AN OVERVIEW*

Denis Steven Rutkus

SUMMARY

In recent decades, the process for appointing judges to the U.S. circuit courts of appeals and the U.S. district courts has been of continuing Senate interest. The responsibility for making these appointments is shared by the President and the Senate. Pursuant to the Constitution's Appointments Clause, the President nominates persons to fill federal judgeships, with the appointment of each nominee also requiring Senate confirmation. Although not mentioned in the Constitution, an important role is also played midway in the appointment process by the Senate Judiciary Committee.

Presidential Selection of Nominees

The need for a President to make a circuit or district court nomination typically arises when a judgeship becomes or soon will become vacant. With almost no formal restrictions on whom the

---

* This is an edited, reformatted and augmented version of a Congressional Research Service, Publication No. R43762, dated October 22, 2014.

President may consider, an informal requirement is that judicial candidates are expected to meet a high standard of professional qualification. By custom, candidates who the President considers for district judgeships are typically identified by home state Senators if the latter are of the President's party, with such Senators, however, generally exerting less influence over the selection of circuit nominees. Another customary expectation is that the Administration, before the President selects a nominee, will consult both home state Senators, regardless of their party, to determine the acceptability to them of the candidate under consideration.

In recent Administrations, the pre-nomination evaluation of judicial candidates has been performed jointly by staff in the White House Counsel's Office and the Department of Justice. Candidate finalists also undergo a confidential background investigation by the FBI and an independent evaluation by a committee of the American Bar Association. The selection process is completed when the President, approving of a candidate, signs a nomination message, which is then sent to the Senate.

Consideration by Senate Judiciary Committee

Once received by the Senate, the judicial nomination is referred to the Judiciary Committee, where professional staff initiate their own investigation into the nominee's background and qualifications. Also, during this pre-hearing phase, the committee, through its "blue slip" procedure, seeks the assessment of home state Senators regarding whether they approve having the committee consider and take action on the nominee.

Next in the process is the confirmation hearing, where judicial nominees engage in a question and answer session with members of the Judiciary Committee. Questions from Senators may focus, among other things, on a nominee's qualifications, understanding of how to interpret the law, previous experiences, and the role of judges.

The committee, when it ultimately votes on a nomination, has three reporting options—to report favorably, unfavorably, or without recommendation. Only on rare occasions has the committee voted to reject a judicial nomination or to report it other than favorably.

Senate Floor Consideration

Customarily, most circuit or district court nominations have reached confirmation under the terms of unanimous consent agreements. On this procedural track, the Senate by unanimous consent not only takes up nominations for floor consideration, but also arranges for them to either receive upor-down confirmation votes or be confirmed simply by unanimous consent. If a roll call vote is asked for, a simple majority of Senators voting, with a minimal quorum of 51 being present, is required to approve a nomination.

For a minority of judicial nominations, however, particularly those facing strong opposition, the procedural track, for moving forward without unanimous consent, customarily has involved the Senate voting on cloture motions to bring floor debate on them to a close. On November 21, 2013, the Senate, by a 52-48 vote, reinterpreted its rules to lower the number of votes needed to close debate on most nominations from three-fifths of the Senate to a simple majority of those voting. Since then, the cloture motion has become the invariable procedural tool used to reach confirmation votes for circuit and district court nominations.

Nominations Not Confirmed

Judicial nominations sometimes fail to be confirmed. This occurs most often when, upon a Senate adjournment or recess of more than 30 days, nominations then in committee or on the Senate's *Executive Calendar* are returned to the President.

INTRODUCTION

Under the Appointments Clause of the Constitution,[1] the President and the Senate share responsibility for making appointments to the Supreme Court, as well as to various lower courts in the federal judiciary. While it is the President who nominates persons to fill federal judgeships, the appointment of each nominee also requires Senate confirmation.[2]

Historically, the vast majority of appointments to judgeships in federal courts other than the Supreme Court have typically not engendered much public disagreement between the President and the Senate and between the parties within the Senate.[3] Debate in the Senate over particular lower court nominees, or over the lower court appointment process, was uncommon, with controversy arising over nominees only on rare occasions. Most such nominations typically were both reported out of committee and confirmed by the Senate without any recorded opposition.

In recent decades, however, appointments to two kinds of lower federal courts—the U.S. district courts and the U.S. circuit courts of appeals—have often been the focus of heightened Senate interest and debate,[4] as has the process itself for appointing judges to these courts.[5] Given congressional interest in the subject, this report is intended to provide readers with a basic overview of the appointment process for U.S. circuit and district court judges. Accordingly, the report, following a brief background section, describes, in successive parts, the three primary phases of the appointment process, namely

- the selection of judicial nominees by the President, including the key role often played by home state Senators in recommending judicial candidates to the President;
- the role of the Senate Judiciary Committee in considering and deciding whether to approve and report out the President's judicial nominations to the Senate; and
- the Senate's floor consideration and confirmation of judicial nominations, through use of either its unanimous consent process or its cloture process.

The report then discusses the final appointment steps for nominees after Senate confirmation, including receipt of commissions signed by the President and the taking of their oaths of office, as well as various possible outcomes for nominees whose nominations are not confirmed, including the possibility of their being re-nominated.

The report's exclusive focus, it should be emphasized, is the process of appointment of U.S. circuit and district court judges *through presidential nomination and Senate confirmation*. This has been, historically as well as in contemporary times, the process by which the vast majority of circuit and district court judges have been appointed. Not analyzed in this report are judicial appointments that occur on rare occasions when a President exercises his constitutional power to make "recess appointments," a process under which an individual can temporarily take office without Senate confirmation.[6]

BACKGROUND AND CONTEXT

The U.S. district courts are the trial courts of general federal jurisdiction, while the U.S. circuit courts of appeals are the intermediate appellate courts that generally consider appeals in cases originally decided by the district courts. With the Supreme Court deciding fewer than 100 cases per term, the district and circuit courts, one scholar has written, "today serve as the final arbiter of more than 99 percent of all federal court litigation," with "important policy ... being made every day in the lower federal courts."[7] Ruling on a wide range of issues, the lower courts, and the persons selected to serve as judges on those courts, arguably have become of much more interest and concern to Congress in recent decades than they were historically.[8]

As congressional interest in the lower federal courts has heightened, the judicial appointment process in turn has often been at the center of Senate debate. In committee and on the Senate floor, Senators periodically have debated over the standards to use in evaluating judicial nominees;[9] over whether certain nominees, if confirmed, would be impartial judges or bring with them ideological agendas or other disqualifying biases;[10] or over how promptly or deliberately to act on judicial nominations.[11]

The judicial confirmation process in the Senate also is longer than it was historically. During the three most recent presidencies (of Bill Clinton, George W. Bush, and Barack Obama), the Senate has, on average, taken much more time to confirm district and circuit court nominees than it did previously—with average times from date of first nomination to confirmation no longer measured in weeks but in multi-month or half-year periods.[12] Perhaps indicative of a more contentious process, the Senate in recent years has been confirming fewer district and circuit nominees by unanimous consent or voice vote than previously, increasingly voting instead by roll call, often with some, and occasionally with a substantial minority of, Senators casting "nay" votes.[13]

Periodically during recent presidencies, the Senate has been divided over whether certain nominations should receive up-or-down confirmation votes. Illustrative of such division have been occasions where motions filed by Senators of the President's party to close debate on particular nominations have, in roll call votes, been opposed, and sometimes defeated, by a substantial number of "nay" votes cast by Senators of the other party.[14]

Frequently, debate over judicial nominations also has centered on the general pace at which the Senate should process the nominations. In a recurring pattern of this debate over recent years, Senators of the President's party, on the one hand, have accused the other party of generally engaging in "obstructionism" or tactics designed to delay or block committee or full Senate action on particular or even relatively large numbers of judicial nominations.[15] Senators of the opposite party, on the other hand, have denied engaging in delaying tactics against judicial nominations, while asserting a Senate duty, under the Constitution's Appointments Clause, to deliberately review the qualifications of judicial nominees rather than to rush or "rubber stamp" the processing of their nominations.[16] Often, in this debate, a related Senate concern has been the number of district or circuit judgeships vacant at that particular time. Senators, along party lines, have differed over whether judicial vacancy levels, when relatively high, were primarily due to delays by the President in making judicial nominations, or to delays by the Senate in confirming them.[17]

Recent frustrations over the judicial appointment process led to a bipartisan agreement reached on January 25, 2013, early in the first session of the 113th Congress. That day, by a 78-16 vote approving S.Res. 15, the Senate established a standing order of the Senate which could accelerate the consideration of nominations, including those to the district courts. The standing order, applicable only in the 113th Congress, significantly reduced (from 30 to 2 hours) the maximum time for consideration of district court nominations after at least three-fifths of the Senate had agreed that debate on the nominations should be brought to a close. The order excluded circuit court nominations (as well as nominations to the Supreme Court, the U.S. Court of International Trade, and major executive branch positions), for which the length of "post-cloture" consideration, under Senate rules, would continue to be 30 hours.[18]

Throughout the rest of 2013, however, the Senate again found itself periodically divided, along party lines, over judicial nominations. At issue was how quickly the Senate should act on lower court nominations in general, and whether or when various circuit court nominations pending on the Senate's *Executive Calendar* should receive confirmation votes.[19] Late in the session, confirmation votes on three circuit court nominations were prevented when motions to close Senate debate on them received only simple majority votes in favor, rather than the three-fifths supermajority then required under Senate rules to close debate.[20] These episodes (along with a simple Senate majority unable again, under similar circumstances, to close debate on an executive branch nomination)[21] set the stage for the Senate's majority leader, shortly thereafter, to put before that body the following issue: Whether, as the majority leader proposed, the Senate should change its procedure to require only a simple majority vote in order to close debate on nominations—thereby more easily reaching confirmation votes, including those on circuit and district court nominations.[22] The proposed procedural change was referred to by some Senate Members, as well as by outside observers and news media reports, as the "nuclear option."[23]

On November 21, 2013, the proposed change in procedure was considered by the Senate. By a vote of 52-48, it overturned a ruling of the chair and set a precedent that lowered the vote threshold required by the Senate for "invoking cloture" (closing debate) on most presidential nominations. Specifically, the Senate reinterpreted the provisions of Senate Rule XXII to require only a simple majority of those voting, rather than three-fifths of the full Senate, to close debate on all presidential nominations except those to the Supreme Court.[24]

Since the November 21, 2013, reinterpretation of its cloture rule, Senate processing of circuit and district court nominations has changed in the following two ways:

- The cloture motion has since become the invariable procedural tool used to reach all confirmation votes for circuit and district court nominations. Before, it generally had been used to close debate on a relatively small number of nominations that did not enjoy wide bipartisan support.[25]
- With a vote threshold needed to close debate lower than it was previously, every motion filed to close Senate debate on a circuit or district court nomination has succeeded—followed in turn by confirmation of each nomination. Before, when the vote threshold was higher, some motions to close debate on judicial nominations were rejected—and the nominations in question blocked from receiving confirmation votes.[26]

As discussed later in this report,[27] it remains to be seen whether the above-noted changes in Senate practice will take a more or less permanent hold, or whether the Senate might, at some point, return to using the unanimous consent process to reach confirmation votes on judicial nominations. Accordingly, given the potential future relevance of both approaches to the Senate, this report, in its discussion of Senate floor consideration of judicial nominations, describes in some detail the two alternate procedural paths that the Senate has taken in recent years when arranging for such nominations to receive confirmation votes.

PRESIDENTIAL SELECTION OF NOMINEES[28]

Court Vacancies Create Need for Judicial Nominations

Federal law authorizes a specific number of full-time active judgeships for each U.S. circuit or district court. The need for a President to make a circuit or district court nomination typically arises when one of these judgeships becomes or soon will become vacant. A judicial vacancy is created by an incumbent judge assuming part-time duties as a "senior status" judge; by a judge's retirement, resignation, or death; or by his or her elevation to a higher court.[29] Judicial vacancies also arise when legislation is enacted creating new judgeships that are to be filled for the first time.

Judges with imminent departure plans frequently give several months of advance notice, permitting the search for judicial replacement candidates to begin even before the vacancy occurs. The stated policy preference of the federal judiciary is that circuit and district court judges intending to leave full-time active status notify the President and the Administrative Office of the United States Courts "as far in advance as possible."[30] (According to the judiciary, over fiscal years 2009 through 2013, the average advance notice provided by outgoing circuit and district court judges ranged from a low of 106 days in FY2009 to a high of 196 days in FY2011.)[31]

Occasionally, a judge also will give notice of the intention to leave office not on a specified future date, but upon the Senate's confirmation of his or her successor. In these circumstances, because of the conditional nature of the outgoing judge's departure, the President's selection of a nominee to succeed the judge necessarily will occur before there is a judicial vacancy.

A complete listing of circuit and district court judgeships which currently are vacant or are scheduled to be vacated in the future is provided on the federal judiciary's website, at http://www.uscourts.gov.[32] The website also maintains a list of judicial vacancies designated as "judicial emergencies" by the Administrative Office of the U.S. Courts. Placed on this list are vacant judgeships located in a district or circuit court deemed to have an extremely high workload or in one that has carried a high workload for an extremely long period of time.[33]

Identification of Judicial Candidates

An Informal Qualification Requirement: Professional Distinction

There are almost no formal restrictions on the potential pool of candidates the President may consider for nomination to circuit or district court judgeships. Neither the Constitution nor any federal statute specifies professional, age, or citizenship requirements for one to be a circuit or district court judge. For appointment to these positions, there "are no exams to pass, no minimum age requirement, no stipulation that judges be native-born citizens or legal residents, and no requirement that judges even have a law degree."[34] Federal law, however, does require (making exceptions for only a few district or circuit courts) that persons at the time of their appointment be residents of the district or circuit and remain so during their judicial service.[35]

Although, as certain scholars have observed, candidates for U.S. judicial posts "do not have to be attorneys—let alone prominent ones—it has been the custom to appoint lawyers who have distinguished themselves professionally (or at least not to appoint those without merit)."[36] Intensive scrutiny of their qualifications is not legally required. It is a well-established practice, however, that candidates for nomination to circuit and district court judgeships are rigorously evaluated for their degree of professional qualification at successive points in the selection process.[37] Expectations that circuit and district court nominees meet a high standard of professional qualification have particularly been fostered by the long-standing role of a committee of the American Bar Association (a role dating back to the early 1950s) in evaluating and rating a President's judicial candidates.[38] Further, virtually every President in recent decades has emphasized the importance of judicial nominees meeting high professional standards, as well as having the ability to be impartial as a judge.

Other Informal Qualification Requirements

Besides the standard of high professional qualification, candidates for district or circuit court judgeships also often have to meet other informal qualification requirements. One such customary requirement usually, if not always, observed is that judicial nominees be of the same party affiliation as the President.[39] Another informal standard generally understood to apply is that judicial candidates have a judicial philosophy, or view of what a judge's fundamental role is in our constitutional system, that is acceptable to the President or to others, such as home state Senators, who might have a deciding role in nominee selection. Scholars also have suggested that in recent decades an informal qualification requirement for judicial candidate has been that their selection be acceptable to the President's political base and to interest groups whose support is important to the President.[40]

Sometimes, a key qualification requirement also will be the ability of a potential candidate to meet a representational standard informally set for the circuit or district court in question. The President (or home state Senators or other state officials recommending judicial candidates to the President) may evaluate the suitability of a candidate according to whether certain groups or constituencies are adequately represented on the court. Among the representational considerations that might be taken into account are a candidate's ethnicity, religion, gender, and place of residence.

The primary role in identifying judicial candidates sometimes is played by the Administration and other times by home state Senators or other officials of the state where the court in question is located. The respective roles that each play often will depend in large part on whether one or both of a state's Senators are of the same party as the President and on whether the candidates are being considered for district or circuit court judgeships.

Identifying District Court Candidates: Role Played by Home State Senators or, Less Often, by Other State Officials[41]

By well-established custom, candidates whom the President considers for nomination to U.S. district court judgeships are identified by U.S. Senators of the state in which the judicial districts are located or by other officials from the state. The President and his Administration rarely initiate the search for district court candidates but instead defer to, and consider only the candidate recommendations made by, home state Senators or other state officials. The role of identifying district court candidates is invariably a senatorial one, if at least one of a state's Senators is of the President's party.[42] By contrast, a home state Senator not of the President's party usually, if not always, plays a secondary rather than primary role in identifying district court candidates.[43]

When One Senator Is of the President's Party

Customarily, Senators of the same political party as the President are the key persons who provide the President's Administration with recommendations for U.S. district court judgeships in their state. One authority on the judicial appointments process has noted that a Senator of the President's party "expects to be able to influence heavily the selection of a federal district judgeship in the senator's state; indeed, most such senators insist on being able to pick these judges."[44]

When only one of a state's Senators is of the President's party, he or she alone, by custom, is entitled to select all candidates for district judgeships in that state. If the Administration has concerns about the Senator's recommendation, it is expected to resolve those concerns with the Senator. If the Administration continues to have a concern over a candidate, finding him or her unacceptable or in some way problematic, the Senator, and not any other official outside the Administration, is called on to provide a different recommendation. Also, by custom, if the Administration prefers its own candidate, it in turn must persuade the Senator to agree to its choice.

When Both Senators Are of the President's Party

If both of a state's Senators are of the President's party, they may share the role of recommending judicial candidates to the President or, alternately, one of them may take the lead role. Senatorial custom, particularly in recent decades, provides ample support for both Senators having an active role in recommending judicial candidates in their states, if each wishes to participate in the process.[45] The extent to which the two Senators will share the judicial role may depend, to a great extent, on their respective prerogatives and interests in this area. If the prerogatives and interests of a state's Senators in selecting judicial candidates are roughly equal (e.g., they are both of the President's party, have about the same amount of Senate seniority, and are both interested in recommending judicial candidates to the President), sharing in some way the candidate selection role seems almost inevitable.

When Neither Senator Is of the President's Party

If neither Senator in a state is of the President's party, each usually, by custom, plays a secondary role in recommending district court candidates for the President's consideration, with the primary role assumed by other officials from the state who are of the President's party.[46] On occasion, however, exceptions do occur, with a President sometimes acquiescing to active senatorial participation in judicial candidate selection in states having two opposition party Senators. On other occasions, an agreed-upon arrangement in a state might be that, while officials of the President's party would be the ones recommending judicial candidates, the state's opposition party Senators would exercise a veto power over any recommendations they found objectionable.

Senators' Involvement in Selection Process Reinforced by Judiciary Committee's Blue Slip Policy

Even when neither of a state's Senators is of the President's party, a consultative role is contemplated, if not mandated, for them in the appointment process by means of the Senate Judiciary Committee's "blue slip" policy. Under this policy, as it has evolved in recent decades,[47] the Judiciary Committee has come to expect that, as a courtesy, a state's Senators, no matter what their party affiliation, will be consulted by the Administration prior to the President nominating persons to U.S. district judgeships in the state as well as to U.S. circuit court judgeships historically associated with their state. Further, under the blue slip policy as applied by various chairs of the Judiciary Committee, a Senator opposed to a judicial nominee from his or her state may—by declining to return a positive blue slip to the committee, or by returning a negative one—block the nominee from receiving a committee hearing or vote.[48] When the blue slip policy is applied in this way, the Administration is well advised, before it selects a nominee, to consult with both home state Senators, regardless of their party, to determine the acceptability to them of a judicial candidate under consideration. To fail to do so is to risk having a nominee unacceptable to a home state Senator vetoed in committee.[49]

How Senators Select Candidates[50]

Senators have great discretion as to the procedures they will follow in identifying and evaluating candidates for appointment to district court judgeships. A Senator may view his or her role in selecting a judicial candidate as essentially making a personal choice, with any input from others being informal in nature. By contrast, as the other end of the spectrum, a Senator may use a formally constituted advisory body of individuals, such as a "nominating commission" or "screening committee," to identify and evaluate judicial candidates.[51] In either case, a Senator's office or nominating commission first may publish notice of the judicial vacancy and invite applications from potential candidates. This typically will be followed by a screening and evaluation process that includes interviews of the most promising candidates by commission members, the Senator's staff, or the Senator. At the end of the process, the Senator will select one or more candidates to recommend to the President for nomination to the vacant judgeship.

Senators might use a number of criteria to determine the fitness of persons from their state to be recommended for district court judgeships. In nearly all cases, a fundamental starting requirement for judicial candidates presumably will be that any person selected have the professional qualifications, integrity, and judicial temperament needed to perform capably as a federal judge. Also, a Senator likely will be guided by at least some political party considerations in the judicial candidate search. (Traditionally, scholars have found, the overwhelming majority of all federal judicial nominees come from the same party as the nominating President.)[52] Further, a Senator may evaluate the suitability of a judicial candidate according to whether certain groups or constituencies are adequately represented on the court in question. A Senator as well may sometimes use normative criteria to evaluate judicial candidates, being concerned, for instance, with what values—legal, constitutional, political, social, economic, and philosophical—would underlie a candidate's reasoning and decision-making as a judge. Since it is the President who ultimately will decide whether a Senator's candidate will be nominated, a Senator might also be expected to take into account any standards explicitly set by the Administration for judicial candidates.

Often a Lesser Role for Senators in Identifying Circuit Court Candidates[53]

Eleven of the 13 U.S. circuit courts of appeals are geographically based courts encompassing three or more states.[54] In each of these circuit courts, many of the seats on the bench have traditionally been linked to a particular state. As a result, Presidents in recent decades usually, but not always, have been inclined to make a circuit court appointment in keeping with the "state seat" tradition by selecting a nominee from the same state as the vacating judge[55]

Senators generally exert less influence over the selection of circuit court nominees than over the selection of district court nominees. Whereas home state Senators of the President's party often, if not always, dictate whom the President nominates to district judgeships, their recommendations for circuit court nominees, by contrast, typically compete with names suggested to the Administration by other sources or generated by the Administration on its own. Indicative of this, an Administration source, early in the Obama Administration, said that President Obama "retained the prerogative" to select circuit court nominees on his own, independently of Senators' recommendations.[56]

While Senators usually are not the dominant or decisive players in the process of selecting circuit court nominees, they, nonetheless, do enjoy certain prerogatives in the process. Once a judgeship in a circuit becomes vacant, Senators in states falling within the circuit are free to suggest names to the Administration regarding possible nominees. If the Administration has indicated which state it wants the judgeship to represent—whether in keeping with a traditional state seat or in a break with that tradition—the Senators of that state, if they are of the President's party, customarily are among those who recommend candidates for the judgeship. Senators of the President's party, one authority has written, "expect judgeships on the federal courts of appeals going to persons from their states to be 'cleared' by them."[57] If the home state Senators are not of the President's party, they nonetheless have expectations—based on the Senate Judiciary Committee's long-standing blue slip policy—that they, too, will be consulted by the Administration for their views about the prospective nominee. A President typically will want to select a circuit court nominee unopposed by both home state Senators, to avoid having a negative or unreturned blue slip from either Senator block the nomination in committee.

Administration Office that Receives Candidate Recommendations

During the presidency of Barack Obama, the White House Counsel's Office has played the primary liaison role with Senators or other state officials regarding judicial appointments (as it did during the presidency of George W. Bush). As the primary consultative link with home state Senators, it is this office that ordinarily receives Senators' recommendations of specific candidates for judicial appointment.[58]

Pre-nomination Evaluation of Judicial Candidates

Vetting by Department of Justice and White House Counsel's Office[59]

In recent presidential administrations, the task of evaluating the background and qualifications of judicial candidates has been apportioned between key staff persons in the White House Counsel's Office and the Department of Justice. These staff, aided by the research of subordinate White House or DOJ personnel, as well as by investigations of the Federal Bureau of Investigation (FBI) into the backgrounds of judicial candidates, decide which candidates to recommend to the President for nomination.

The evaluation process of various candidates under consideration for nomination to a judgeship often involves a "preliminary vetting." In this initial vetting phase, Administration staff may interview some or all of the candidates (either by phone or in person) and review publicly available information about them (such as their published writings and news media accounts of their past activities in public life). The candidates also might be asked to fill out various forms and questionnaires, including a personal background information form for the FBI, a financial disclosure form, and a White House or Senate Judiciary Committee questionnaire. (In other cases, however, the Administration might wait until it has narrowed down the nominee search to one candidate, requiring only that candidate to fill out such forms.) After the evaluation process is narrowed down to one person (or after a single initial candidate passes the initial vetting phase), the candidate is recommended for more intensive evaluation to the President, who, if he agrees, clears the candidate for "detailed vetting."

For its part, detailed vetting may move forward on different fronts. Administration staff can be expected to carefully review the candidate's written opinions or other legal writings (depending on whether the candidate is a judge or a practicing attorney), as well as the forms and questionnaires filled out by the candidate. If they have not already done so, they likely will now interview the candidate in person, as well as persons in the legal community who have had past contact with, or have knowledge about, the candidate. The FBI will conduct a confidential background investigation of the candidate, which typically takes four to six weeks.[60]

Evaluation of Candidate by ABA Committee

The detailed vetting stage may also provide for evaluation of the judicial candidate by a committee of the American Bar Association. The committee which performs this evaluation, the ABA's Standing Committee on the Federal Judiciary, is made up of 15 lawyers with various professional experiences.[61] Since 1953, every presidential Administration, except that of George W. Bush, has sought ABA pre-nomination evaluations of its candidates for district and circuit court judgeships.[62]

The stated objective of the ABA committee is to assist the White House in assessing whether prospective judicial nominees should be nominated.[63] It seeks to do so by providing what it describes as an "impartial peer-review evaluation" of each candidate's professional qualifications. This evaluation, according to the committee, focuses strictly on a candidate's "integrity, professional competence and judicial temperament" and does not take into account the candidate's "philosophy, political affiliation or ideology." In evaluating professional competence, the committee assesses the prospective nominee's "intellectual capacity, judgment, writing and analytical abilities, knowledge of the law, and breadth of professional experience."[64]

Evaluation of the judicial candidate is usually assigned to the ABA committee member from the judicial circuit in which the judicial vacancy exists. The committee evaluator assesses the qualification of the candidate in the following ways:

- by examining the candidate's responses to a comprehensive Personal Data Questionnaire, forwarded to the committee by the Department of Justice;

- by examining the candidate's legal writings and reviewing reported court decisions, briefs, legal memoranda, publications, speeches, hearing and argument transcripts, articles, and other writings by or involving the candidate;
- by conducting extensive confidential interviews of a broad cross section of judges, lawyers, and others who have served, or had other professional contact, with the candidate, to obtain their assessments of his or her integrity, professional competence, and judicial temperament; and
- by interviewing the candidate near the end of the evaluation process, affording him or her "a full opportunity to address and rebut any adverse information or comments" that might have come to the evaluator's attention during the evaluation process.[65]

After completing the above steps, the evaluator prepares an informal report for the committee chair. The report, in evaluating the candidate's professional qualifications, rates the candidate as either "well qualified," "qualified," or "not qualified." After reviewing the informal report for thoroughness, the committee chair informs the White House of "the likely outcome of the evaluation" by the full committee. If the White House requests the process to continue (which it typically does if the candidate has received an informal report rating of "qualified" or better), the chair directs the evaluator to prepare a formal report.[66] After independently reviewing the formal report, each member of the committee votes on which rating category the candidate should receive. Once all votes are tallied, the chair confidentially advises the White House of the committee's rating, including whether the committee vote for it was unanimous.[67] The rating will remain confidential and not be disclosed publicly until the candidate is nominated by the President. If the candidate is not nominated, the rating is not publicly released.[68]

Conveyed to the White House on a confidential basis, the ABA committee rating becomes part of a judicial candidate's overall profile for the Administration to consider in the pre-nomination evaluation process. On the one hand, a "well qualified" or "qualified" rating by all or a substantial majority of the committee's members typically may be seen by the Administration to strengthen the case for a candidate's nomination. On the other hand, a "not qualified" rating may be a reason for the President not to nominate. In such instances, another pre-nomination consideration is that the "not qualified" rating, and the reasons for it, will be publicly disclosed if the candidate is nominated. (In keeping with standard ABA committee practice, if a candidate is nominated in spite of a majority "not qualified" rating, the reasons for this rating will be made public if the Senate Judiciary Committee holds a hearing on the nomination.[69] By contrast, it is not ABA committee practice to explain to the Judiciary Committee its reasons for any other ratings, including split votes in which a minority of committee members rate a nominee "not qualified.")

ABA committee evaluations of judicial candidates, it should be stressed, are provided to the Administration strictly on an advisory basis. It is solely in the President's discretion as to how much weight to place on a judicial candidate's ABA rating in deciding whether to nominate. Hence, a "not qualified" ABA rating of a judicial candidate in some instances may dissuade a President from nominating,[70] while in other instances the President may nominate in spite of the rating.[71] Likewise, a favorable "well qualified" or "qualified" ABA rating of a judicial candidate does not oblige a President to nominate, and a President for his own reasons sometimes may choose not to nominate such a candidate.

Staff Recommendation, Then Nomination by the President

Near the end of detailed vetting, judicial selection staff in the Administration may, if necessary, conduct follow-up interviews of the candidate (either in person or by telephone) to address any new questions or confirm new information arising out of the detailed vetting process. Finally, Administration staff will evaluate the results of the detailed vetting effort and formally recommend to the President whether to nominate the candidate. If the recommendation is to nominate, and it meets with presidential approval, the President will sign a nomination message, which is then sent to the Senate.

Obama Administration Selection of Lower Court Nominees: A Chronology of Usual Steps

In an article published in the summer of 2013, three political scientists examined in detail the selection and confirmation processes of U.S. circuit and district court judges during President Obama's first term.[72] Their examination, the scholars noted, relied on extensive interviews with officials in the Department of Justice (DOJ), the White House Counsel's Office, and Senate staff personnel.[73] Their narrative description of judicial selection within the Obama Administration, they said, focused in particular on the roles played by the White House Counsel's Office and the Office of Legal Policy in the DOJ. From their narrative,[74] CRS has culled, in bullet points, the following chronology of steps described by the authors as usually taken by the Administration in selecting circuit or district court nominees:

- White House Counsel's Office receives nominee recommendations from home state Senators; for each district court vacancy, the office asks Senators to send three recommendations.[75]
- Senators send one or more recommendations to the Counsel's Office.
- Counsel's Office does preliminary check of the recommended candidates, then selects one to be thoroughly vetted by the Department of Justice's Office of Legal Policy (OLP).[76]
- OLP does detailed vetting of the candidate, including exhaustive reading of candidate's past writings, speeches, interviews, etc., and making "about 25 to 50 phone calls."
- Counsel's Office and OLP jointly interview the candidate.
- Counsel's Office and OLP jointly review OLP's detailed vetting and interview record and decide whether to send candidate's name for ABA and FBI investigations.
- FBI and ABA's Standing Committee on the Federal Judiciary conduct separate evaluations of the candidate and then report their findings to the Administration.
- OLP and Counsel's Office sign off informally on the candidate.
- President selects the candidate for nomination.

CONSIDERATION BY SENATE JUDICIARY COMMITTEE

The President customarily transmits a circuit or district court nomination to the Senate in the form of a written nomination message. Once received, the nomination is numbered by the Senate executive clerk, read on the floor, and then immediately referred to the Judiciary Committee.[77]

The committee will play a key role, as an intermediary between the President and the full Senate, in deciding whether the nomination ultimately moves forward in the confirmation process. For the long-established Senate practice is that the Judiciary Committee must act on—and specifically "report"—a circuit or district court nomination before the whole Senate can act on it.[78]

The Judiciary Committee's processing of the nomination typically consists of three phases—a pre-hearing phase, the holding of a hearing on the nomination, and voting on whether to report the nomination to the Senate.

Pre-Hearing Phase

Upon referral of a judicial nomination to the Judiciary Committee, professional staff on the committee initiate an investigation into the nominee's background and qualifications. Nominations units for the majority and the minority staff, each with their own nominations counsel, clerk, and investigators, will do their own research and review of the background of the nominee. Resources closely examined in their investigation will be a committee questionnaire completed by the nominee and any documents concerning the nominee provided by the Administration. The pace and timing of the staff investigation of the nominee may also depend on whether, or how promptly, home state Senators return their blue slips to the committee. Of interest as well to the committee's pre-hearing evaluation will be the ABA rating that the nominee receives.

Committee Questionnaire

One primary source of information for staff review will be the committee's "Questionnaire for Judicial Nominees," to which each nominee responds in writing. The questionnaire asks the nominee for detailed biographical and financial disclosure information, including a comprehensive listing of the nominee's published writings, speeches, and activities in law, politics, and academia.[79] If, as often is the case, the nominee has filled out the questionnaire prior to being nominated, the Administration will be able provide the questionnaire to the Judiciary Committee within days of the nomination being made. For its part, the committee expects the nominee to complete the questionnaire before it will hold a hearing on the nomination.

A chief purpose of the questionnaire is to provide members of the Judiciary Committee and their staffs with detailed pre-hearing information about the nominee, thereby better equipping the committee to gauge the professional qualifications of the nominee. The completed questionnaire also can be helpful to the committee in identifying new questions that Senators might have about the nominee's background and therefore want to pose at his or her hearing.

The committee typically treats the questionnaire's biographical and financial disclosure sections as public information.[80] The committee, however, treats as confidential (and not available to the news media or the public) the nominee's responses to more sensitive questions, such as whether he or she ever had been under investigation for possible violation of a civil or criminal statute.[81]

As one political scientist has observed, the committee questionnaire, including its financial disclosure sections, "have become a routine part of the confirmation process," with nominees expected to "respect the importance of the documents" and be fully responsive to their questions.[82] In the event a nominee discovers something omitted from the initial questionnaire, he or she is expected to provide the committee, as soon as possible, with follow-up supplemental questionnaire responses.[83]

Administration Documents

The Judiciary Committee also may receive documents concerning the nominee from the White House, the Department of Justice, and the Federal Bureau of Investigation. Confidential FBI reports on the nominee are an important and regular source of background information for the committee. These reports are available only to committee members, a small number of designated staff, and home state Senators.[84] (The reports are distinct from the records of FBI investigations, which are provided only to the White House.) The reports, a scholar has noted, ordinarily "do not provide damaging information about nominee," but "in a small number of cases, the material may require the committee to look further into a matter of concern."[85]

Blue Slips from Home State Senators

During the pre-hearing phase, the committee also formally solicits the opinions that home state Senators have of judicial nominees. Under its long-standing blue slip procedure, the chair of the Judiciary Committee seeks the assessment of home state Senators regarding circuit and district court nominees to judgeships within or associated with their state, including whether they approve having the committee consider and take action on the nominee. The chair does this by sending a blue-colored form to the Senators regarding the nominations.[86] Through return of the blue slip to the committee, the committee's website has noted, home state Senators "can approve moving the nominee through the Committee process."[87] Conversely, however, a home state Senator may prevent committee consideration of the nomination if he or she decides not to return the blue slip or to return it with a negative response.

Recent chairs of the Judiciary Committee have required a return of a positive blue slip by both Senators in a state delegation before allowing a nomination to advance in the committee process.[88]

ABA Rating

Also of interest to the Judiciary Committee is the rating that each circuit and district court nominee receives from the American Bar Association's Standing Committee on the Federal Judiciary. The chair of the ABA committee provides formal notification of this rating in a letter to the chair of the Judiciary Committee, typically soon after the person is nominated.[89] The letter tells the Judiciary Committee whether the nominee received a "well qualified," a "qualified," or (on rare occasions) a "not qualified" rating, and whether the ABA committee members were unanimous in their rating. If the rating is not unanimous, the letter will indicate whether a "majority" or "substantial majority" of committee members voted in favor of it.[90]

The ABA committee also, after informing the Judiciary Committee, makes its ratings of the judicial nominee available to the public, on its website, at http://www.americanbar.org/groups/ committees/federal_judiciary.html. On the website, a ratings chart for nominees in the current Congress is updated regularly, while ratings for nominees in earlier Congresses (dating back to the 101st Congress) are also available online.

The ABA committee letter informs the Judiciary Committee only of the nominee's ABA rating, without providing any explanation of the rating. If the nominee received either a unanimous or majority "well qualified" or "qualified" rating, the Judiciary Committee will receive no further information from the ABA committee concerning the rating. Likewise, in the event that a minority of the ABA committee's members rated a nominee "not qualified," their reasons for doing so will not be provided to the Judiciary Committee prior to, at, or after the nominee's confirmation hearing.[91]

By contrast, in the rare instance where a nominee receives either a unanimous or majority "not qualified" rating, the ABA committee will submit a written statement to the Judiciary Committee explaining the rating. The statement, however, ordinarily will be submitted to the committee only 48 hours in advance of the nominee's confirmation hearing.[92] (The chair of the ABA committee also will testify at the confirmation hearing to further explain, and answer questions about, the committee's rating.)

A nominee's ABA rating will be one among many factors for the Judiciary Committee to consider in its pre-hearing investigation of the nominee's judicial qualifications. At the outset, a unanimous "qualified" or higher rating may be considered, by its very nature, a plus for the nominee, with the nominee's fitness to be a judge attested to by the ABA committee's peer review evaluation. On the other hand, a "not qualified" rating, or even a split vote by the ABA committee with a minority rating the nominee "not qualified," might raise questions for the Judiciary Committee to investigate further in its pre-hearing investigation of the nominee.

Length of Pre-hearing Phase

The pre-hearing phase for a circuit or district court nominee may extend over a period of months. There is variation across presidencies (as well as Congresses) in the length of time that circuit and district court nominees wait, on average, to receive a hearing after being nominated by a President.[93]

How quickly a lower court nominee will receive a confirmation hearing may be affected by a variety of factors. These factors may include, but not be limited to (1) how quickly the committee's questionnaire is filled out and provided to the committee; (2) the volume of investigative information there is about the nominee for committee staff to review and analyze; (3) whether any controversy surrounds the nominee; (4) partisan or ideological differences over judicial nominations between the President and the party of the Judiciary Committee's majority or minority; and (5) the inclination of the committee chair as to when to schedule a confirmation hearing.

The scheduling of a confirmation hearing for a circuit or district court nominee is at the discretion of the chair of the Judiciary Committee. Under the committee's rules, the committee must provide public announcement of any hearing at least seven calendar days prior to the start of the hearing (unless the chair and ranking minority Member "determine that good cause exists to begin the hearing at an earlier date").[94] Such notice is posted on the Judiciary Committee's website at http://www.judiciary.senate.gov.

Hearing Phase

At a confirmation hearing, lower court nominees engage in a question and answer session with members of the Senate Judiciary Committee. The hearing typically is held for more than one judicial nominee at a time. In such situations, the hearing sometimes may consist of two consecutive panels—for example, one panel for several district court nominees, followed by another for a circuit court nominee.

Dynamics of the Hearing

At the hearing, either the chair of the Judiciary Committee, or another committee member delegated the task, will preside. Each judicial nominee will be "presented," or introduced, to the committee by one or both of his or her home state Senators. (Sometimes as well a senior House member or other state official may make a statement in support of the nominees.[95])

The presiding Senator, after calling the hearing to order, may make a short introductory statement. He or she will then invite the presenters to make their statements in support of the nominees. After this, the nominees will make brief opening statements (which typically include noting the presence at the hearing of family members and friends). Then, the hearing begins in earnest, with Senators on the committee posing questions to each nominee. The questions, it has been noted,

> ... typically address the individual's qualifications, understanding of how to interpret and apply the law, previous experiences in court, judicial temperament, and the role of judges. However, the Committee's members are not limited to these topics and may ask about anything contained in the Committee questionnaire. In essence, the nominee should be prepared to speak to the entirety of his/her legal career, writings, and speaking engagements.[96]

Most confirmation hearings for circuit and district court nominees, a scholar has observed, are not attended by all members of the Judiciary Committee.[97] If a Senator does not attend, others have noted, "it is likely that his or her staff will, and will report back to the senator."[98] (While the committee's quorum requirement for a hearing is only one Senator,[99] typically at least one committee member of the minority party is present along with the presiding Senator at confirmation hearings for district court nominees, with a greater number of Senators of both parties typically in attendance for a hearing on a circuit court nominee.)

Sometimes, however, confirmation hearings may prove less routine, particularly if there are concerns among committee members about a nominee's qualifications. In such an event, the questioning of a nominee may be more intensive or extended than otherwise, and more Senators than usual may attend to engage in the questioning. Further, if a nominee is relatively controversial, a hearing occasionally may be held exclusively for that nominee. On rare occasions, the committee may hold more than one day of hearings on a lower court nomination, if such additional time is considered needed for adequate questioning of the nominee.

While a confirmation hearing is a means for the Judiciary Committee to evaluate a judicial nominee firsthand, it also, a scholar has suggested, serves a public education function (with the committee's website making available to the public a live webcast of each hearing). As well, it affords judicial nominees an opportunity to address any concerns that Senators might have about them.[100]

Statements from Public Witnesses

The confirmation hearing may also receive statements from public witnesses. Typically, if not always, these statements, whether in support of or in opposition to the nominee, will be written submissions. For example, if the nominee received a positive ABA rating, the Judiciary Committee's published hearing record will include only a letter attesting to that rating from the ABA's Standing Committee on the Federal Judiciary—rather than any oral testimony about that rating from an ABA spokesperson. Likewise, any statements to the Judiciary Committee by local or state bar associations or interest groups, either for or against the nominee, usually are submitted only in written form, rather than by in-person testimony. Sometimes, as well, the Judiciary Committee may receive written statements, rather than testimony, concerning a nominee from Senators not on the committee (usually home state Senators).[101]

In some instances, however, public witnesses may testify in person. This occurs, for instance, on the rare occasions when a lower court nominee has received a negative ABA rating. In these instances, the chair and another member of the ABA committee customarily appear at the confirmation hearing to explain the rating and answer any questions that Senators on the Judiciary Committee may have about it. Also, the committee sometimes, though infrequently, has permitted in-person testimony by public witnesses speaking for and against confirmation when nominees have been highly controversial.

Follow-up Questions

After the hearing, circuit or district court nominees sometimes may be required to provide written responses to follow-up questions from Senators on the Judiciary Committee. In some instances, Senators may pose these questions at the hearing, for a nominee to reply to afterwards. In other instances, Senators at the hearing may request that the nominee reply to a list of written questions that they will provide after the hearing. Follow-up questions often raise issues that Senators were unable to bring up at the hearing due to time constraints or other reasons, or they may ask the nominee to elaborate on responses he or she provided to certain questions at the hearing. Written responses to these questions, the Judiciary Committee has indicated, are necessary before the committee will consider whether to report the nomination to the Senate.[102] The nominee's written responses will be included in the public record of the hearing that is subsequently published by the Government Printing Office.

Hearings on judicial nominations are not required under the rules of the Senate or the Judiciary Committee. As noted earlier, whether or when a hearing will be held on a circuit or district court nominee is at the discretion of the committee's chair. At the same time, it is well-established practice of the Judiciary Committee that it will not vote on whether to report a circuit or district court nominee without having first held a hearing on the nominee.[103] Some nominations, therefore, will fail to advance to the committee reporting stage if the Chair, for a policy or other reason, decides against scheduling a hearing. (The hearing, for example, might not be held because a home state Senator has declined to return a blue slip, or because the nomination was referred to the committee with little time left in the congressional session.)

Sometimes, however, judicial nominees who fail to receive a hearing on their first nomination receive a hearing on a later nomination to the same court. For example, a nominee's first nomination, under Senate rules, may be returned to the President upon a Senate recess or adjournment of more than 30 days, only to have the person involved later re-nominated by the President. Hearings on second nominations also are particularly common for judicial nominees initially nominated late in a Congress and then re-nominated by the President early in the next Congress.[104]

Typically, for a circuit or district court nominee who receives a hearing, there will be only one hearing—even if he or she were nominated more than once. The Judiciary Committee, in other words, typically will not require a new hearing for a re-nominated judicial nominee who already received a hearing on a previous nomination (for instance, during the previous Congress). An additional hearing for a nominee, however, may always be held if new circumstances are perceived by the committee to warrant one.

Committee Reporting Phase

At the beginning of this phase, the nomination awaits a vote by the Judiciary Committee on whether it should be reported to the Senate as a whole. A committee vote in favor of reporting is the crucial step needed to send the nomination forward to the Senate. Conversely, if the nomination is not put to the committee for a vote, or if the committee votes against reporting it, the nomination will not move forward, ultimately failing to receive Senate confirmation.

Scheduling a Vote on the Nominee

Decisions of whether or when to schedule judicial nominations for vote in committee are made by the committee's chair. Nominees slated for this vote are publicly listed in the agenda for the committee's next scheduled business meeting.[105] The meeting itself, when it occurs, typically will, in line with recent committee practice, be webcast live from the committee. After the fact, a link on the committee website will list the results of the meeting (including whether and how the committee voted on judicial nominations).

When the meeting of the Judiciary Committee is held, a sufficient number of members must be present for the committee to report a nomination. The committee's rules provide that no nomination (or bill or matter) "shall be ordered reported ... unless a majority of the Committee is actually present at the time such action is taken and a majority of those present support the action taken."[106]

If quorum requirements are met, the chair may then move or ask for unanimous consent that the nominations on the agenda either individually or en bloc be ordered reported to the Senate. It is not uncommon, however, for such votes to be delayed (or "held over") by one business meeting, at the request of a committee member (usually, if not always, of the committee minority). This comports with committee rules, under which any Senator on the committee may delay the vote by one committee business meeting or for one week, "whichever occurs later."[107] It is at the chair's discretion as to whether to honor requests to delay a nomination over longer periods.

Reporting Options

The committee, when it ultimately votes on the nomination, has three reporting options—to report favorably, unfavorably, or without recommendation. Almost always, when the committee votes on a nomination, it votes to report favorably. The committee, however, may vote (as it has done in the past, but only on rare occasions) to report unfavorably or without recommendation.[108] Such a vote advances the nomination for Senate consideration despite the lack of majority support for it in committee.

The Judiciary Committee may vote on a motion to report a judicial nomination either by voice vote or by roll call. Historically, in the vast majority of cases (if not all cases), votes on motions to report district or circuit court nominations have been by voice vote. In recent years, however, with committee members more frequently requesting the yeas and nays, roll call votes on judicial nominations have become somewhat more common.[109] Motions to gain approval in Senate committees require a majority vote in favor and thus fail if there is a tie vote.

Nominations That Die in Committee

In contrast to nominations reported to the Senate, some lower court nominations never leave the committee and die there. This occurs most dramatically when the Judiciary Committee votes against reporting a nomination. Historically a rare occurrence, a majority vote against reporting is an explicit act of rejection by the committee that also serves to prevent the nomination from receiving Senate consideration.[110] However, the much more common way in which a nomination dies in committee is for it to fail ever to receive committee action. In most such cases, the nomination, having not advanced out of committee, is, under Senate rules, returned to the President when the Senate adjourns or recesses for more than 30 days, or at the final adjournment of a Congress.[111] Also, on infrequent occasions, judicial nominations have failed when, while in committee, they were withdrawn by the President.[112]

Under Senate rules, it might be noted, a judicial nomination pending in the Judiciary Committee could also reach the Senate floor without being reported out of committee—if the Senate agreed to discharge the committee from consideration of the nomination.[113] As a CRS report observes, it is "fairly common for committees to be discharged from noncontroversial nominations by unanimous consent, with the support of the committee, as a means of simplifying the process."[114] Nonetheless, in a database search of judicial nominations dating back to the mid-1940s, CRS research has identified no instances in which the Senate has discharged the Judiciary Committee of a judicial nomination.[115]

SENATE FLOOR CONSIDERATION

Executive Calendar and Going into Executive Session to Take Up a Nomination

After it is reported by the Judiciary Committee, a circuit or district court nomination is listed on the *Executive Calendar*, with a number assigned to it by the Senate's executive clerk. On this calendar, the nomination joins a list of other nominations (judicial and executive branch), as well as treaties, that have been reported out of committee and are eligible for floor consideration.[116] (The *Executive Calendar* is separate from the Senate's *Calendar of Business*, which lists pending bills and resolutions.) The nominations are listed chronologically according to the date each was reported. The *Executive Calendar* provides basic information for each nomination, including the nominee's name and office, the name of the previous holder of the office, and when the committee reported the nomination.[117] In the rare instance that a committee has reported a nomination unfavorably or without recommendation, instead of favorably, that information is supplied as well.[118]

The *Executive Calendar* is published each day the Senate is in session and distributed to Senate personal offices and committee and subcommittee offices. It is also available to congressional personnel online by following the link to *Executive Calendars* under the "Senate" tab of the website of the Legislative Information System of the U.S. Congress.[119]

Business on the *Executive Calendar,* including a circuit or district court nomination, is considered by the Senate in executive session. While the Senate usually begins the day in legislative session, it subsequently enters executive session either by a non-debatable motion or, far more often, by unanimous consent. By custom, most motions and requests to go into executive session to consider a judicial or other nomination are made by the Senate majority leader.[120] Under Senate rules, the nomination cannot be taken up until it has been on the *Executive Calendar* at least one calendar day.[121]

Two Alternate Procedural Tracks Followed by Senate in Confirming Lower Court Nominations

In practice, Senate floor consideration of circuit or district court nominations follows one of two procedural tracks. Customarily, most of these nominations, particularly if uncontroversial, have reached confirmation under the terms of unanimous consent agreements. On this procedural track, the Senate by unanimous consent not only takes up nominations for floor consideration, but also arranges for them to either receive up-or-down confirmation votes or be confirmed simply by unanimous consent.

For other judicial nominations, however, particularly those facing strong opposition, unanimous consent to reach confirmation may not always be attainable. In these instances, the procedural track, for a nomination to move forward without unanimous consent, involves the Senate, after taking up the nomination, voting on a cloture motion to bring floor debate to a close. If the requisite majority under Senate rules supports closing debate, a confirmation vote on the nomination must be held after a limited period for consideration.

For many decades until late into the first session of the 113th Congress, the Senate used unanimous consent agreements to decide how and when to act on the vast majority of circuit and district court nominations that ultimately were confirmed. However, the routine use of the unanimous consent process in confirming lower court nominations ended after the Senate, on November 21, 2013, reinterpreted paragraph 2 of Senate Rule XXII, also known as the "cloture rule." In reinterpreting the rule, the Senate lowered the number of votes needed to close debate on nominations, other than to the Supreme Court, from three-fifths of the Senate to a simple majority of those voting.[122] Hence, under the reinterpreted rule, a simple majority of Senators, by voting in favor of a motion to close debate on a circuit or district court nomination, could compel a Senate vote on confirmation—something that, prior to the rule's reinterpretation, would occur only if a three-fifths supermajority voted in favor of cloture.

Since the Senate's November 21, 2013, reinterpretation of Rule XXII, floor practice in confirming circuit and district court nominations has changed in the following way: Votes on confirmation, even for uncontroversial nominations, are no longer reached by unanimous consent, but instead by the cloture process. Used primarily in the past to close debate on a relatively small number of nominations that did not enjoy wide bipartisan support, the cloture motion has now become the invariable procedural tool used to reach confirmation votes for all circuit and district court nominations. It remains to be seen whether this fundamental change in Senate practice will take a more or less permanent hold, or conversely whether the Senate, at some future point, might return to its traditional reliance on the unanimous consent process to confirm most judicial nominations.

The following paragraphs discuss in more detail the manner in which circuit and district court nominations reach confirmation on the Senate floor, depending on whether unanimous consent or cloture is the procedural track taken. Descriptions of Senate procedures draw from relevant CRS reports as well as from research for this report that examined Senate floor treatment of judicial nominations over a 27-year period (starting with the 100th Congress (1987-1988) and carrying up to the current 113th Congress).[123]

Unanimous Consent Agreement to Vote on or Confirm a Judicial Nomination

Senate floor consideration of a judicial nomination by unanimous consent (UC) typically is scheduled by the majority leader in consultation with the minority leader and with all interested Senators. The majority leader, in such consultation, seeks to establish that, if requested on the floor, no Senator will object to the nomination receiving a vote on confirmation. If this can be established, the leader will make the unanimous consent request at a convenient agreed-upon time.

The UC request usually, if not always, is made while the Senate is in legislative session. In making the request, the majority leader (or, in some instances, another Senator acting on behalf of the majority leader) asks for unanimous consent to proceed to executive session—immediately, at some specified future time, or at a time to be determined later by the majority leader—to consider and then vote on the nomination.

UC Agreements with Time Limits Prior to Vote

The unanimous consent request might or might not provide for debate prior to the Senate voting on the nomination. If providing for debate, the UC request usually includes a time limit for the debate and sometimes as well a set time on which the nomination will receive a Senate vote. Typically, the amount of time for debate is divided evenly between the majority and minority parties, who usually have as their respective floor managers the chair and ranking minority Member of the Judiciary Committee. If agreed to, a time limit on debate forecloses the use of unlimited debate or other tactics to delay or prevent a vote on the nomination.

When there is debate on a circuit or district court nomination, the chair of the Judiciary Committee usually makes an opening speech, often followed by remarks by the committee's ranking minority Member. One or both of a judicial nominee's home state Senators often may speak on the nominee as well, particularly if they were involved in the selection process.

At the end of debate, the presiding officer puts the following question before the Senate: "Will the Senate advise and consent to the nomination of [the judicial nominee in question]?" If no Senator asks for a roll call vote, the Senate may approve the nomination by voice vote. In other instances, however, a roll call vote will be taken on the nomination if any Senator present "asks for the yeas and nays."[124] A simple majority of Senators voting (with a minimal quorum of 51 being present) is required to approve a nomination.

Roll call votes on judicial nominees scheduled for a vote by unanimous consent may be close or lopsided. In recent decades, such roll calls have ranged from Senators voting unanimously in favor of confirmation to other instances with more than a third of Senators present voting against.[125] Hence, a UC agreement to vote on a judicial nomination does not always indicate the absence of Senate opposition to the nominee; however, it does mean that, in instances where some Senators will oppose confirmation, they have not objected, but rather have agreed (through unanimous consent), to the Senate voting on the question of whether to confirm.

UC Agreements to Confirm without Debate or Vote

Sometimes, a unanimous consent request may ask for the Senate to proceed immediately to executive session to consider and confirm particular judicial nominations, without providing for any debate on them or for a vote by Members on whether to confirm. Such a request may be for consideration and confirmation of a single nomination or of an "en bloc" group of nominations. (For instance, the request, if involving several nominations, might ask both that the Senate proceed to consider the nominations and that they "be confirmed en bloc.") If the request is agreed to, the nomination or nominations are confirmed immediately, upon the presiding officer stating, "Without objection, it is so ordered." UC agreements to confirm without debate or vote, in the absence of any objection to confirmation, typically involve only judicial nominations on which no Senator wishes to record formal opposition.

Unanimous consent sometimes also is requested for the Senate to proceed only to consideration of a nomination, without further providing for a vote on confirmation. This typically indicates that the majority leader, or other Senator making the request, anticipates an objection would be raised on the floor to an up-or-down confirmation vote. Although the request falls short of bringing the nomination to a vote, it places the nomination on the floor for it to be championed by Senate supporters in executive session, leaving open the option for supporters to make another UC request for a confirmation vote at a later time.[126]

More frequently, however, a UC request to proceed to consider a judicial nomination, without also requesting a Senate vote, serves a different strategic purpose: By bringing the nomination to the floor, it sets the stage for Senate supporters to try to use the cloture process to force a vote on confirmation, a process described next in this report.

Reaching a Vote on Confirmation through the Cloture Process

As discussed above, historically the usual route to confirmation for circuit and district court nominations has been for Senate floor votes on confirmation to be scheduled by unanimous consent. The Senate, however, has not always been able to agree unanimously on whether or when certain judicial nominations (often because of controversy associated with the nominees) should receive up-or-down votes. Further, since November 21, 2013, when it reinterpreted its rules for ending debate on most nominations, the Senate has not been able to use the UC process to schedule a confirmation vote on any circuit or district court nomination. Since then, only a few UC requests for the Senate to consider and then vote on such nominations have been made, with objection heard to each request.[127]

Without Time Limit on Nomination, Senate Rules Permit Unlimited Debate

A nomination under floor consideration without a time agreement for a vote is, under Senate rules, susceptible to being blocked indefinitely by opponents. That is because, as a CRS report has noted, "Senate rules place no general limits on how long consideration of a nomination (or most other matters) may last. Owing to this lack of general time limits, opponents of a nomination may be able to use extended debate or other delaying actions to prevent a final vote from occurring."[128]

As long as at least one Senator is understood to be opposed to a nomination receiving a confirmation vote, an objection can be expected if unanimous consent is requested for that purpose.[129] As a result, the procedural track, if the nomination is to move forward to a vote in the absence of unanimous consent, will involve the Senate voting on a motion for cloture (the motion to bring floor debate to a close).[130]

Presenting Motion to Close Debate on a Nomination

Before such a motion can be filed, the Senate must be considering the nomination. To get to this point, unanimous consent ordinarily would be requested (or less frequently, a non-debatable motion made) that the Senate go into executive session to consider the nomination.[131] Once the Senate has agreed to take up the nomination, a cloture motion to close debate can be made. Under the cloture rule (paragraph 2 of Senate Rule XXII), at least 16 Senators must sign a cloture motion. Typically, in recent years, the cloture motion has been sent to the desk immediately after the nomination has been taken up, although it can be done at any time the nomination is under Senate consideration.[132] The motion, which is read by the clerk, states that the "undersigned Senators, in accordance with the provisions of Rule XXII of the Standing Rules of the Senate, hereby move to bring to a close debate on" the nomination.

Voting on the Cloture Motion

Passing of Two Session Days for Cloture Motion to "Ripen"

The Senate, unless deciding otherwise by unanimous consent, will not vote on the cloture motion until the second day of session after the motion has been presented. For example, if the motion were presented on a Monday, the Senate would act on it on Wednesday. (During the two days of session that elapse prior to the cloture vote, the Senate can and typically does turn to other business.)

Typically, on the day the cloture motion "ripens," a unanimous consent agreement will provide for a specified period of time for debate, divided equally between the two parties, immediately prior to the cloture vote. Then, at the appointed time, with the Senate in executive session, Senators will vote either yea or nay on the question, "Is it the sense of the Senate that debate ... shall be brought to a close?"

Cloture Invoked by Simple Majority Voting in Favor

Pursuant to the November 21, 2013, decision of the Senate, cloture can be invoked in the Senate on most nominations, including circuit and district court nominations, by a simple majority of Senators voting in favor, a quorum being present. (Prior to that decision, dating back to 1975, it took three-fifths of the Senate, or 60 Senators if no more than one Senate vacancy, voting in favor of the motion to invoke cloture on a nomination.)

"Post-Cloture" Time, after Cloture Is Invoked

If cloture is invoked, under Rule XXII, there can be, prior to the Senate voting on confirmation, a maximum of 30 hours of consideration for circuit court nominations (including debate and time consumed by quorum calls, parliamentary inquiries, and all other proceedings).[133] Pursuant to a standing order of the Senate, nominations of district court judges during the 113th Congress are subject to a lower, 2-hour maximum of post-cloture consideration.[134] (This post-cloture time is equally divided and controlled by the majority and minority, which means all or some of the controlled time may be "yielded back" by either side.) In future Congresses, however, "the post-cloture consideration limits will revert back to 30 hours for all nominations, unless the Senate provides otherwise."[135]

After cloture is invoked, a frequent practice of the Senate (even when closely divided over whether to confirm a nominee) is to proceed to a vote on confirmation without debating the nomination for the maximum amount time allowed prior to the vote. This may be achieved by UC agreements that, for instance, yield back all or most "post-cloture" time prior to the scheduled votes on confirmation,[136] count time during adjournment or recess as post-cloture time,[137] or use large blocks of time, leading up to the confirmation vote, for consideration of legislative or other business unrelated to the nomination.[138] When all post-cloture time has expired or been yielded back, the Senate then takes up the question of whether to confirm the nomination. As previously noted, the vote threshold by which the Senate can confirm is a numerical majority of those voting (provided a quorum is present).

Sometimes, the majority leader files multiple cloture motions on judicial nominations in a single day, to allow the motions to ripen simultaneously. In order to do so, the majority leader must first bring each nomination to the floor, and then file cloture on each one, a process that is usually expedited by unanimous consent.[139] Two days of session later, the Senate votes on cloture on the first nomination. Assuming cloture is invoked, the Senate would then consider the nomination under the applicable time limit. After the time expires, the Senate would vote on confirmation. Then the cloture motion on the second nomination would be voted on. In the case of district court nominations, which at least for the 113th Congress are considered for a maximum of two hours post-cloture (half of which can be yielded back by the majority), the Senate can invoke cloture and confirm multiple nominations in a single day.[140] The processing of cloture motions and confirmation votes on multiple nominations may be expedited by UC agreements limiting or dispensing with time for post-cloture debate as well as those limiting time for voting on the nominations themselves.[141]

If a Cloture Motion Is Rejected

If a cloture motion is rejected, a nomination remains on the *Executive Calendar* (unless it is withdrawn by the President or returned to the President at the start of a recess of more than 30 days). During the remainder of the Congress, supporters are free, if they wish, to file additional cloture motions on the nomination (a relatively rare occurrence).[142] Ultimately, however, the nomination, if not confirmed before the final adjournment of the Congress, is returned to the President at that time.

Pre-November 21, 2013—Cloture Motions Filed on Small Share of Judicial Nominations

As noted above, prior to November 21, 2013,[143] it took three-fifths of the Senate, or 60 Senators if there were no more than one vacancy, to invoke cloture on a nomination. Typically, in recent decades, cloture motions were filed to limit debate on only a small share of the judicial nominations taken up for floor consideration.[144] One disincentive to their more frequent use was the super-majority vote required to invoke cloture. For example, supporters of a blocked circuit court nomination might have declined to file a cloture motion, anticipating that less than three-fifths of the Senate would vote in favor of closing debate. Also, greater floor time was required to confirm judicial nominations through the cloture process than by unanimous consent agreements—time which arguably the Senate might often have preferred to devote to other business than judicial nominations.

Post-November 21, 2013—Cloture Motions Invoked on All Confirmed Judicial Nominations

By contrast, since the Senate's November 21, 2013, decision to require only a simple majority to invoke cloture on most nominations, all confirmations of circuit and district court nominations in the 113th Congress have been reached through the cloture process. Since then, the process for every confirmed circuit or district court nomination has involved the filing of a cloture motion, and the Senate then voting to invoke cloture, prior to a confirmation vote. All but a few of the votes invoking cloture during this period have involved majorities of less than three-fifths of the Senate in favor of closing debate (voting majorities falling short of the number required to invoke cloture prior to November 21, 2013).[145] During this period, no confirmations of circuit or district court nomination have been reached through the unanimous consent process. As noted earlier, requests for unanimous consent to confirm or vote on circuit and district court nominations have been made on only a handful of occasions, with objections heard to each request.

While it is more time-consuming to reach judicial confirmations using the cloture process than by unanimous consent, the Senate sometimes, in conjunction with the cloture process, uses UC agreements to shorten the time required to confirm nominations. These include agreements, concerning nominations on which cloture has been invoked, to limit or "yield back" post-cloture time, to count time during adjournments or recesses as post-cloture time, and to reduce the time ordinarily allowed for roll call votes on whether to confirm.[146]

Use of Roll Call Votes to Confirm Nominations

As noted earlier, the Senate may confirm nominations by unanimous consent, voice vote, or by recorded roll call vote. When the question of whether to confirm a nomination is put to the Senate, a roll call vote will be taken on the nomination if the Senate has ordered "the yeas and nays." (The support of 11 Senators is necessary to order the roll call.)[147]

Historically, the Senate has confirmed most district and circuit court nominations by unanimous consent or by voice vote. In recent decades, however, confirmations by roll call votes have become more common, and during the presidencies of George W. Bush and Barack Obama, they have been the most common way that the Senate has confirmed lower court nominations.

A relatively small percentage of President Ronald Reagan's and George H.W. Bush's lower federal court nominees received Senate confirmation by roll call vote. According to CRS data, 5 (or 6.0%) of President Reagan's 83 confirmed circuit nominees and only 1 (2.4%) of H.W. Bush's 42 circuit court nominees were approved by roll call votes.[148] Additionally, only 1 district court nominee was confirmed by roll call vote during the Reagan presidency,[149] and no district court nominees were confirmed by roll call votes during H.W. Bush's presidency.

Confirmation by roll call vote became more common during William J. Clinton's presidency, with 16 (24.6%) of 65 confirmed circuit court nominees and 32 (10.5%) of 305 confirmed district court nominees receiving Senate roll call votes. It was not, however, until President George W. Bush's tenure that a majority of lower court nominees were approved by roll call votes, with 49 (80.4%) of 61 circuit court nominees and 141 (54.0%) of 261 district court nominees confirmed in this way. This trend has continued under President Obama, with 47 (88.7%) of 53 confirmed circuit court nominees receiving roll call votes and 147 (65.9%) of 223 district court nominees receiving roll call votes (as of October 1, 2014).[150] Since the Senate's reinterpretation of the application of Senate Rule XXII on November 21, 2013, all U.S. circuit and district court nominations have been approved by recorded roll call vote.[151]

After Confirmation of a Nomination

Reconsideration

Senate Rule XXXI provides that, after the Senate has confirmed a nomination, any Senator who voted with the majority has the option of moving to reconsider the vote. Only one motion to reconsider is in order on the nomination, and it must be made on the day of the vote or on one of the next two days the Senate meets in executive session. Typically, however, the Senate, before the vote on confirmation has occurred, preempts the motion to reconsider, arranging beforehand by unanimous consent for it to be considered tabled in the event the nomination is confirmed. It is typical, for example, for the Senate, in a unanimous consent time agreement for a confirmation vote on a circuit or district court nomination, to include the provision that, after the vote, "the motion to reconsider be considered made and laid upon the table." Similarly, UC agreements concerning upcoming cloture votes on nominations often provide for the tabling of the motion to reconsider in the event cloture is invoked and the nominee then confirmed. In either case, tabling the motion prevents any subsequent attempt to reconsider.[152]

Resolution of Confirmation

With the motion to reconsider tabled, the Secretary of the Senate attests to a resolution of confirmation and transmits it to the White House. (In the rare instance of the Senate voting against confirmation, the Secretary will transmit to the President a resolution of disapproval.) Senate Rule XXXI requires that the Secretary wait until the time for moving to reconsider has expired before notifying the President that a nomination has been confirmed. Such notice, however, in practice "is usually sent immediately, permitted by unanimous consent."[153]

Post-Senate Appointment Steps

President Signs Commission[154]

Upon notification of a nominee's confirmation, the President performs the next step in the appointment process—the signing of the nominee's commission. The commission is a formal document empowering the nominee to assume the judicial office, which the President must sign before the nominee may begin his or her new duties. The date of a nominee's commission is the date the President signs it, which usually occurs within a few days of Senate confirmation (but can also occur on the same date as the confirmation itself). The commission is transmitted to the Department of Justice, which then sends it, as well as a packet of other documents, to the nominee.

Oath of Office

The appointment commission packet sent by the Department of Justice includes various forms to accompany the statutory oath of office, which each circuit and district judge must take before exercising the judicial authority of the United States. The oath of office is orally administered by someone legally authorized by state or federal law to administer oaths, including the chief judge or another judge on the court to which the nominee is assuming his or her position. Additionally, in some cases, the home state Senator of a nominee has administered the oath of office. The oath is a combination of the judicial oath of office required of every Justice and judge of the United States under 28 U.S.C. 453 and the general oath administered to all federal government officials, set forth in 5 U.S.C. 3331.[155]

At the time the oath of office is executed, the nominee himself or herself must also sign and date the commission. If two or more confirmed nominees to the same court sign their commissions on the same date, seniority is determined by seniority of age of the nominees. If, for example, Judges A and B both sign on the same date and Judge A is older than Judge B, then Judge A is considered more senior than Judge B.[156]

This process—receipt of the packet from the Department of Justice, administering the oath of office to the nominee, including obtaining his or her signature on the commission—typically occurs within a week or two of Senate confirmation. In some cases, however, a nominee might wait longer, for professional reasons, to take the oath and sign his or her commission. For example, a law professor who is confirmed as a U.S. district court judge might wait to sign her commission until after she has finished teaching for the semester.

Investiture

Typically, the last step in the appointment process is the investiture. At this ceremonial event, attended by family and friends, the new judge is sworn in yet again, in the courtroom. The ceremony, however, is not required for the nominee to assume office and can take place weeks or months after the oath of office is executed.[157]

NOMINATIONS NOT CONFIRMED

Typically, during any given Congress, some circuit and district court nominations fail to receive Senate confirmation. How far along in the confirmation process they progress will vary. Some may not receive any committee consideration, while others might advance through part but not all of the committee stage (for example, receiving a hearing without being reported); still others, after being reported by committee, may be placed on the *Executive Calendar* without, however, receiving Senate floor consideration, or in other cases receive floor consideration but not a vote on confirmation. A variety of factors might play a part in a nomination's failure to advance farther, including the extent of Members' support for, or opposition to, the nomination and scheduling considerations and competing demands on the Judiciary Committee's or the Senate's time (often problematic for nominations the President sends to the Senate relatively late in a Congress).

For judicial nominations that fail to be confirmed, the appointment process ends with one of three possible steps—rejection by the Senate (very rare), withdrawal of a nomination by the President (occasional, but infrequent), and (by far the most common occurrence) Senate return of the nomination to the President at the end of a session, at the end of the Congress, or upon a recess of more than 30 days. Although the appointment process is finished for such nominations, the President (or a successor President) is not precluded from re-nominating a person. In fact, when a circuit or district court nomination is returned, the nominee often is re-nominated and eventually confirmed.[158]

Rejection by the Senate

A lower court nomination, after advancing through nearly the entire confirmation process, only very rarely is then rejected by the full Senate. Over a 75-year period researched by CRS, from 1939 to the present, only six instances were found of the Senate, in a floor vote on confirmation, rejecting a district court nomination, while none was found of the Senate rejecting a circuit court nomination.[159] (As noted earlier, when the Senate votes against confirmation, that action is followed immediately by the Secretary of the Senate transmitting to the President a resolution of disapproval.)

Withdrawal of Nomination by the President

Occasionally, for a judicial nomination that fails to be confirmed, the final step in the appointment process consists of the President withdrawing the nomination. (The President does this by transmitting to the Senate a message of withdrawal.) A nomination may be withdrawn for a variety of reasons. It might, for example, be withdrawn because prospects for its confirmation are viewed as unfavorable; there is no longer presidential support for it; the nominee has requested the withdrawal; or the President wishes to re-nominate the nominee to a different judgeship. Typically, during a presidency, only a small number of circuit or district court nominations are withdrawn.[160]

Return of Nominations to the President

Under Senate Rule XXXI, paragraph 6, all pending nominations (whether in committee or on the *Executive Calendar*) are returned to the President when the Senate adjourns *sine die* at the end of a session or when it recesses for more than 30 days. The return of a nomination to the President marks its end point in the appointment process, with its final status that of an unconfirmed nomination. However, nominations sometimes are not returned, if the Senate elects to waive the above rule. Further, even when a nomination is returned, the President has the option of renominating (i.e., sending to the Senate a new nomination of) the person in question, and this option is often exercised.

Rule for Return of Nominations Often Waived by Senate

At the end of a Congress, all pending nominations must be returned to the President, in keeping with Rule XXXI, paragraph 6. However, on other occasions, when adjourning between sessions or recessing for more than 30 days, the Senate often waives the rule by unanimous consent. (It commonly does so, for instance, before adjourning for its August or its inter-session recess.) In waiving the rule, the Senate, instead of returning nominations to the President while in recess, allows them to remain "in status quo."

A UC agreement to have nominations remain pending in status quo during long recesses, however, may not always cover all nominations. Sometimes instead, if one or more Senators oppose the continued pendency of certain nominations, these specifically will be excluded from the agreement, necessitating their return to the President during the recess.[161]

President May Re-nominate Unconfirmed Nominees

When the Senate returns a nomination, the President ordinarily has only two options—to select a new nominee or to re-nominate, staying with the person previously nominated. Presidents frequently choose to do the latter, sending to the Senate new nominations of their previous nominees. On occasions when the Senate, at the start of a long recess, sends back all or nearly all pending nominations (having not reached a UC agreement for such nominations to remain in status quo), the President typically, without hesitation, re-nominates all or nearly all of the nominees involved. (A few possible exceptions might be made, and new nominations not submitted, for persons regarded as having doubtful chances for confirmation.)

By contrast, as already noted, the Senate sometimes may return only a few judicial nominations, having, by unanimous consent, agreed that all other nominations remain in status quo during the long recess. The return of only certain specified nominations often may be an indicator to the President of some degree of opposition in the Senate to the nominations. As such, it is, in the case of each nomination, a consideration for the President to weigh in deciding whether to re-nominate or to select a new nominee.

Following the return of all pending nominations at the final adjournment of a Congress, a President, early in the next Congress, is free to re-nominate persons whose previous judicial nominations were returned.[162] However, even if some of the previous nominations progressed through certain steps of the confirmation process (for instance, they were reported out of committee or received floor consideration), the new nominations will have to repeat some of the steps taken previously in order to be processed and confirmed, in the new Congress. The new nominations, for instance, will again be referred to the Judiciary Committee and must be approved by the committee in order to be placed on the *Executive Calendar.* At the committee's discretion, however, one formal step in the confirmation process—the confirmation hearing—is sometimes dispensed with if a judicial nominee already received a hearing in the previous Congress and an additional hearing is considered unnecessary.[163]

End Notes

[1] Article II, Section 2, clause 2 of the Constitution—often referred to as the Appointments Clause—provides that the President "shall nominate, and by and with the Advice and Consent of the Senate, shall appoint ... Judges of the supreme Court, and all other Officers of the United States, whose Appointments are not herein otherwise provided for, and which shall be established by Law.... "

[2] The Constitution also, in its Recess Appointments Clause (Article II, Section 2, clause 3) authorizes the President to make temporary appointments unilaterally during periods when the Senate is in recess. In recent decades, however, Presidents have rarely used their recess appointment authority to appoint federal judges. A CRS report notes that while historically it was not uncommon for Presidents to make recess appointments to the federal judiciary, in "recent years, recess appointments of federal judges have been unusual and controversial." Over the past 25 years, the report adds, "there have been only three recess appointments to fill federal judgeships to Article III judgeships"—one such appointment to a circuit court judgeship by President William J. Clinton in 2000 and two to circuit court judgeships by President George W. Bush in 2004. CRS Report RS21308, *Recess Appointments: Frequently Asked Questions*, by Henry B. Hogue.

[3] In this vein, one scholar has noted that, relative to Supreme Court appointments, appointments to the lower federal courts "have not, for most of our history, engaged remotely similar public interest. Nor as a historical matter has the Senate played the same role in considering nominations to those courts." Stephen B. Burbank, "Politics, Privilege & Power; The Senate's Role in the Appointment of Federal Judges," *Judicature*, vol. 86 (July/August 2002), p. 25.

[4] In an early indication at the committee level of this heightened interest, the then-chair of the Senate Judiciary Committees, Senator Edward M. Kennedy, in 1979 "greatly strengthened the existing investigative procedures by assigning additional committee staff to conduct background checks on judicial nominations." This was followed, in the mid-1980s, by the "first known instance of the minority party in the Judiciary Committee establishing its own investigative unit, and beginning to closely review nominations." Mitchel A. Sollenberger, *Judicial Appointments and Democratic Controls* (Durham, NC: Carolina Academic Press, 2011), pp. 105-106.

[5] For discussion by scholars of the Senate's increased interest in the judicial appointment process in recent decades see Nancy Scherer, *Scoring Points; Politicians, Activists, and the Lower*

Federal Court Appointment Process (Stanford, CA: Stanford University Press, 2005), 271 p. (Hereafter cited as Scherer, *Scoring Points.)* See also Sarah A. Binder and Forrest Maltzman, *Advice & Dissent: The Struggle to Shape the Federal Judiciary* (Washington: Brookings Institution Press, 2009), p. 198 p. For two relatively recent forums in which numerous Senators in detailed statements expressed their views concerning the lower court appointment process, see U.S. Congress, Senate Committee on the Judiciary, Subcommittee on Administrative Oversight and the Courts, *The Judicial Nomination and Confirmation Process*, Hearings, 107th Cong., 1st sess., June 26 and Sept. 4, 2001, S.Hrg. 107-463 (Washington: GPO, 2002), 276 pp.; and U.S. Congress, Senate Committee on the Judiciary, Subcommittee on Constitution, Civil Rights and Property Rights, *Judicial Nominations, Filibusters, and the Constitution: When a Majority Is Denied Its Right to Consent*, Hearing, 108th Cong., 1st sess., May 6, 2003, S.Hrg. 108-227 (Washington: GPO, 2003), p. 393 pp.

[6] As noted above, in footnote 2, judicial recess appointments in recent decades have been rare and, like recess appointments to other positions, have been controversial when perceived as a way for Presidents to appoint officials who might otherwise have difficulty securing Senate confirmation. The Senate during recent Congresses periodically has used pro forma sessions that prevented the occurrence of recesses of more than three days during which the President might make recess appointments. In January 2012, the President made four non-judicial recess appointments during one of these brief recesses between two pro forma sessions of the Senate, and this action was challenged in federal court. The Supreme Court, at the end of its 2013-2014 term, ruled, in part, that the President may not make recess appointments when the Senate is convening every three days for a pro forma session. Arguably, the congressional scheduling practices, together with the Court's ruling, have limited the scope of the President's authority to make future recess appointments. For more on congressional efforts to block recess appointments, see CRS Report R42329, *Recess Appointments Made by President Barack Obama*, by Henry B. Hogue and Maureen O. Bearden. For more on the Supreme Court decision, see CRS Report RL33009, *Recess Appointments: A Legal Overview*, by Vivian S. Chu.

[7] Scherer, *Scoring Points,* p. 19.

[8] See, for example, Roger E. Hartley and Lisa M. Holmes, "The Increasing Senate Scrutiny of Lower Federal Court Nominees," *Political Science Quarterly*, vol. 117, no. 2 (Summer 2002), pp. 259-278;also, Jennifer A. Dlouhy, "Parties Use Judicial Standoff to Play to Core Constituents," *CQ Weekly*, vol. 60 (October 19, 2002), pp. 2722-2726.

[9] See, for example, U.S. Congress, Senate Committee on the Judiciary, Subcommittee on Administrative Oversight and the Courts, *The Judicial Nomination and Confirmation Process*, Hearings, 107th Cong., 1st sess., June 26 and September 4, 2001, S.Hrg. 107-463 (Washington: GPO, 202), pp. 1-276.

[10] See, for example, Charles Lane, "Judicial Nominee Challenged on Abortion Views," *The Washington Post*, July 24, 2002, p. A4; Neil A. Lewis, "Democrats on Senate Panel Pummel Judicial Nominee," *The New York Times*, March 2, 2005, p. A18; Seth Stern, "GOP: Liu's Nomination to 9th Circuit is 'in Jeopardy'," *CQ Today Online News*, April 6, 2010, at http://www.cq.com; and Joanna Anderson, "Judiciary Committee Approves Contentious Nomination for Appellate Court," *CQ Today Online News*, June 10, 2010, at http://www.cq.com.

[11] See, for example, David Ingram, "Slow Going in Senate for DOJ, Judicial Nominees," *The National law Journal*, vol. 32 (January 4, 2010), pp. 17, 20; Jessica Brady, "Three Judicial Confirmations Generate Debate on Senate's Pace," *Roll Call*, June 7, 2010, p. at http://www.rollcall.com..

[12] See CRS Report R43369, *U.S. Circuit and District Court Nominations During President Obama's First Five Years: Comparative Analysis With Recent Presidents*, by Barry J. McMillion (under heading "Length of Time from Nomination to Confirmation"). See also Benjamin Wittes, *Confirmation Wars; Preserving Independent Courts in Angry Times* (Lanham, MD: Bowman & Littlefield, 2006), pp. 38-39 (noting that from 1945 to 1980 the norm was for the Senate to confirm lower court judges in less than a month and from 1981 to 1986 to do so between one month and two).

[13] See "Figure 6. U.S. Circuit and District Court Nominees of Five Most Recent Presidents (January 20, 1981, to May 31, 2012): Percentage of Confirmed Nominees Approved by Roll Call Votes," in CRS Report R42556, *Nominations to U.S. Circuit and District Courts by President Obama During the 111th and 112th Congresses*, by Barry J. McMillion.

[14] For a full list, from 1968 through 2012, of Senate votes on motions to close debate on judicial and other nominations, including votes rejecting such motions, see CRS Report RL32878, *Cloture Attempts on Nominations: Data and Historical Development*, by Richard S. Beth.

[15] See, for example, the floor remarks of Sen. Patrick J. Leahy, in: "Unanimous Consent Request—Executive Calendar," *Congressional Record*, daily edition, vol. 156 (July 20, 2010), pp. S6011-S6013; "Nomination of Jane Margaret Triche-Milazzo," *Congressional Record*, daily edition, vol. 157 (October 11, 2011), pp. S6376-S6377; and "Executive Session," *Congressional Record*, daily edition, vol. 159 (March 11, 2013), pp. S1280-S1282.

[16] See, for example, the floor remarks of Sen. Jeff Sessions, in "Judicial Nominations," *Congressional Record*, daily edition, vol. 156 (September 22, 2010), pp. S7314-S7317; also, the floor remarks of Sen. Chuck Grassley, in "Nomination of Jane Margaret Triche-Milazzo," *Congressional Record*, daily edition, vol. 157 (October 11, 2011), pp. S6375-S6376 and in "Executive Session," *Congressional Record*, daily edition, vol. 159 (March 11, 2013), pp. S1282- S1283.

[17] See CRS Report R41942, *Vacancies on Article III District and Circuit Courts, 1977-2011: Data, Causes, and Implications*, by Denis Steven Rutkus (especially under heading "Recent Historical Background").

[18] See CRS Report R42996, *Changes to Senate Procedures at the Start of the 113th Congress Affecting the Operation of Cloture (S.Res. 15 and S.Res. 16)*, by Elizabeth Rybicki (under heading "Reduced Post-Cloture Consideration for Nominations (Section 2 of S.Res. 15)"); also, Niels Lesniewski, "Senate Opens with Filibuster Changes," *CQ Weekly*, vol. 71 (January 28, 2013), p. 216.

[19] See, for example, Niels Lesniewski, "Going 'Nuclear'? Democrats Ratchet Up Talk on Judicial Picks," *CQ News*, April 8, 2013, at http://www.cq.com; Humberto Sanchez, "Senate Democrats Set Showdown over Filibusters of Nominees," *CQ Weekly*, vol. 71 (July 15, 2013), p. 1212; and Eliza Newlin-Carney, "The Senate's Standoff Culture," *CQ Weekly*, vol. 71 (July 22, 2013), pp. 1252-1253..

[20] The three nominations on which the Senate rejected motions to close debate were all to the U.S. Court of Appeals for the District of Columbia Circuit. Specifically, the Senate rejected: on October 31, 2013, by a roll call vote of 55 yeas to 38 nays, a motion to close debate on the DC circuit nomination of Patricia Ann Millett of Virginia; on November 12, 2013, by a roll call vote of 56 yeas to 41 nays, a motion to close debate on the DC circuit nomination of Cornelia T. L. Pillard of the District of Columbia; and on November 18, 2013, by a roll call vote of 53 yes to 38 nays, a motion to close debate on the DC circuit nomination of Robert Leon Wilkins of the District of Columbia. (In each case, with three-fifths of the

Senate's 100 Members not having voted in the affirmative, the "cloture motion" was not agreed to.)

[21] On October 31, 2013, the Senate, by a roll call vote of 54 yeas to 42 nays, rejected a motion to close debate on the nomination of Melvin L. Watt of North Carolina to be Director of the Federal Housing Finance Agency.

[22] See Meredith Shiner, "Reid: 'We Need to Do Something' After GOP Filibusters of Nominations," *CQ News*, November 19, 2013, at http://www.cq.com; Humberto Sanchez, "Reid Moves Closer to Triggering Filibuster Rules Fight Over Nominations." *CQ News*, November 19, 2013, at http://www.cq.com.

[23] See, for example, Stephen Dinan, "Rule-Changing 'Nuclear Option' May Be Getting Close," *The Washington Times*, November 19, 2013, p. A3. As a CRS report has noted, some Senators and outside observers have used the term "nuclear' to describe proceedings that "might rely on steps that are novel (potentially in contravention of existing rules and precedents) or because they could undermine the prerogatives exercised heretofore by Senate minorities or individual Senators." CRS Report R43331, *Majority Cloture for Nominations: Implications and the "Nuclear" Proceedings*, by Valerie Heitshusen.

[24] "Appealing Ruling of the Chair," Senate debate, *Congressional Record*, daily edition, vol. 159 (November 21, 2014), p. S8418. (See pp. S8414-8418, for debate and procedural votes that preceded the vote to overturn the ruling of the chair) and pp. S8419-S8428, for remarks immediately thereafter of various Senators commenting on the significance of the new precedent approved by the Senate.) See also CRS Report R43331, *Majority Cloture for Nominations: Implications and the "Nuclear" Proceedings*, by Valerie Heitshusen, for analysis of the procedural context of the Senate's November 21, 2013 actions and for a detailing of the key procedural steps taken by the Senate that day to lower the vote threshold required for invoking cloture on most presidential nominations.

[25] See section in this report under heading "Senate Floor Consideration."

[26] Ibid.

[27] See discussion in this report under heading "Two Alternate Procedural Tracks Followed by Senate in Confirming Lower Court Nominations."

[28] This report section, it should be noted, applies to the nominee selection process for judgeships in the U.S. district courts geographically located within the nation's 50 states and in the 11 geographically based U.S. circuit courts that, in each case, comprise three or more states. A significant aspect of that selection process, as discussed herein, involves the key role often played by home state Senators. This aspect of the selection process, however, would not apply to the selection of judicial nominees to certain federal district courts not located in a state or to the two U.S. circuit courts that do not geographically consist of states. (The federal district courts not located in a state are the U.S. District Court for the District of Columbia, the U.S. District Court for the District of Puerto Rico, and the territorial district courts in the U.S. Virgin Islands, Guam, and the Northern Mariana Islands. The two U.S. circuit courts not geographically consisting of states are the U.S. Court of Appeals for the District of Columbia and the U.S. Court of Appeals for the Federal Circuit.) A description of each of these courts' nominee selection processes (including a discussion of which kinds of officials, in the absence of home state Senators, might play a key role in influencing the President's selection of nominees) is outside the scope of this report.

[29] A vacancy also would occur if Congress removed a judge through the impeachment process, but historically such occurrences have been extremely rare. A CRS report issued in 2011 noted that "only 12 impeachment trials [of judges] have been completed over the 222-year history of the Senate, while three others terminated before a determination on the merits of

the case due to the resignation of the judges in question." CRS Report R41172, *The Role of the Senate in Judicial Impeachment Proceedings: Procedure, Practice, and Data*, by Betsy Palmer.

[30] In March 2003, the federal judiciary's governing body, the Judicial Conference of the United States, adopted a committee recommendation, in which it "strongly urge[d] all judges to notify the President and the Administrative Office of the United States Courts as far in advance as possible of a change in status, preferably 12 months before the contemplated date of change in status." Prior to that, retiring judges and those taking senior status had been encouraged by the Conference to provide "substantial (i.e., six-month or one-year) advance notice of that action." U.S. Judicial Conference of the United States, *Report of the Proceedings of the Judicial Conference of the United States*, March 18, 2003, pp. 20-21, at http://www.uscourts.gov/FederalCourts/JudicialConference/Proceedings/Proceedings.aspx?doc=/ uscourts/FederalCourts/judconf/proceedings/2003-03.pdf.

[31] Data on the average length of notice that full-time circuit and district court judges gave before taking senior status, resigning, or retiring, by fiscal year, were provided to CRS, on request, by the Office of Legislative Affairs, Administrative Office of the U.S. Courts.

[32] Within the website, a list of current circuit and district court vacancies can be accessed at http://www.uscourts.gov/JudgesAndJudgeships/JudicialVacancies/CurrentJudicialVacancies.aspx A list of future court vacancies (including, for each judgeship in question, the date that the vacancy will take effect) can be accessed at http://www.uscourts.gov/ JudgesAndJudgeships/Judicial Vacancies/FutureJudicialVacancies.aspx.

[33] The list of vacant circuit or district court judgeships designated by the federal judiciary as "judicial emergencies" can be accessed at http://www.uscourts.gov/JudgesAnd Judgeships/JudicialVacancies/JudicialEmergencies.aspx.The website list also explains what workload and judgeship vacancy time data are used by the Judicial Conference to determine whether a vacant district or circuit court judgeship is defined as a "judicial emergency."

[34] Robert A. Carp, Ronald Stidham, and Kenneth L. Manning, *Judicial Process in America*, 6th ed. (Washington: CQ Press, 2004), p. 121. (Hereinafter cited as Carp et al., *Judicial Process*.)

[35] See "Statutory Qualifications for Judicial office," in Mitchel A. Sollenberger, *Judicial Appointments and Democratic Controls* (Durham, NC: Carolina Academic Press, 2011), pp. 52-68.

[36] Carp et al., *Judicial Process*, p. 121.

[37] For instance, where Senators are engaged in identifying and recommending judicial candidates, the candidates, in many cases may be evaluated or rated by a local or state bar association or some other kind of informal or formal panel of lawyers called upon specifically to evaluate the candidate's professional qualifications. A judicial candidate, too, will be closely investigated by Administration personnel involved in advising the President on whether the candidate should be nominated. The nominee's qualifications also will be exhaustively examined by the American Bar Association' Standing Committee on the Federal Judiciary, either in the selection process prior to nomination or immediately after the nomination is made. Finally, the nominee will be scrutinized yet again, by staff of the Senate Judiciary committee, upon Senate receipt of the nomination from the President.

[38] See archived CRS Report 96-446, *The American Bar Association's Standing Committee on Federal Judiciary: A Historical Overview*, by Denis Steven Rutkus. (Available from author.)

[39] This tradition, particularly with regard to selecting district court candidates, is linked to political patronage concerns of home state Senators of the President's party. See discussion

of "political qualifications" that often are said to play a part in the selection of federal judicial nominees, including "the fact that well over half of all federal judges were politically active before their appointments," in Carp et al., *Judicial Process*, pp. 122-123.

[40] See, for example, Scherer, *Scoring Points*, pp. 49-73.

[41] The discussion under this heading is taken largely from CRS Report RL34405, *Role of Home State Senators in the Selection of Lower Federal Court Judges*, by Barry J. McMillion and Denis Steven Rutkus (specifically, report section "Senators' Party Affiliations and Their Recommending Role").

[42] While the President, pursuant to the Constitution's Appointments Clause, retains the nominations power exclusively, the role of Senators in identifying candidates for district court judgeships in their states by custom dates back to the early 19th Century. One scholar, writing in 1953, described what was then the "well-established custom which has prevailed since about 1840," wherein U.S. district judges "are normally selected by senators from the state in which the district is situated, provided they belong in the same party as the President." Joseph P. Harris, *The Advice and Consent of the Senate* (Berkeley, CA: University of California Press, 1953); reprint, New York: Greenwood Press, 1968, pp. 40-41 (page citation here is to the reprint edition).

[43] For further discussion of the role during the current Obama Administration of home state Senators in selecting, or otherwise influencing the President's selection of, candidates for district court judgeships in their state, see Sheldon Goldman, Elliot Slotnick, and Sara Schiavoni, in "The Confirmation Drama Continues," *Judicature*, vol. 94, no. 6 (May/June 2011), pp. 266-269, and in "Obama's First Term Judiciary; Picking Judges in the Minefield of Obstructionism," *Judicature*, vol. 97, no. 1 (July/August 2013), pp. 16-18.

[44] Sheldon Goldman, "Judicial Selection," in Robert J. Janosik, ed., *Encyclopedia of the American Judicial System: Studies of the Principal Institutions and Processes of Law*, 3 vols. (New York: Scribner, 1987), vol. 2, p. 589. (Hereinafter cited as Goldman, in *Encyclopedia of American Judicial System.*)

[45] Indicative of this custom were the findings of a survey in early 1993, during the first months of Democrat William J. Clinton's presidency, of staff in Senate offices on methods used to select candidates for district judgeships. At that time, 18 states were represented by two Democratic Senators. Of these 18 states, 11 were identified in the survey as having both of their Senators jointly involved in the selection of judicial candidates, while in five other states one of the Senators was identified as the "chief sponsor" or as "taking the lead" in the selection process. (In the two other states, the Senators had yet to decide on what selection process they would use.) *Citizen's Handbook Supplement: A State-byState Guide to Federal Judicial Selection* (Washington: Alliance for Justice, April 1993), 15 p. (Copy of pamphlet available from author.)

[46] For example, in a state without a Senator of the President's party, the role of recommending judicial candidates to the President might be performed by the state's most senior U.S. Representative of the President's party, by the party's House delegation as a whole, or by the state's governor, if of the President's party..

[47] See archived CRS Report RL32013, *The History of the Blue Slip in the Senate Committee on the Judiciary, 1917- Present*, by Mitchel A. Sollenberger.

[48] See "Blue Slip Policy of Senate Judiciary Committee" and "Should the Policy of the Judiciary Committee allow a Home State Senator to Block Committee Consideration of a Judicial Nominee?" in CRS Report RL34405, *Role of Home State Senators in the Selection of Lower Federal Court Judges*, by Barry J. McMillion and Denis Steven Rutkus.

[49] For a recent statement by the current chair of the Senate Judiciary Committee in support of a blue slip policy requirement of clearance from both home state Senators in order for judicial nominations to move forward in committee, see Sen. Patrick J. Leahy, "'Blue Slips' Help Make Constitutional Advice and Consent' a Reality," statement for release to press, April 7, 2014, at http.//www.leahy.senate.gov.

[50] The discussion under this heading draws largely from CRS Report RL34405, *Role of Home State Senators in the Selection of Lower Federal Court Judges*, by Barry J. McMillion and Denis Steven Rutkus (specifically, from sections under report headings "Procedures Used to Identify and Evaluate Candidates" and "Criteria Used to Select Judicial Candidates").

[51] For thumbnail descriptions of the structure and operations of nominating commissions currently used by Senators in the federal judicial selection process in certain states, see "Federal Judicial Selection" link on American Judicature Society's "judicial Selection in the States" website, at http://www.judicialselection.us/federal_judicial_selection/ federal_judicial_nominating_commissions.cfm?state=FD, For a guide designed to provide Senators, other federal legislators, and their staffs with information about creating committees to screen potential judicial nominees, see The Governance Institute, Governance Studies at Brookings, and the Institute for the Advancement of the American Legal System, *Options for Federal Judicial Screening Committees: Where They Are in Place, How They Operate, and What to Consider in Establishing and Managing Them*, second ed., September 2011, 37 p., at http://iaals.du.edu/library/ publications/options-for-federal-judicial-screening-committees-second-edition.

[52] Carp et al., *Judicial Process*, p. 122; Sheldon Goldman, Elliot Slotnick, and Sara Schiavoni, "Obama's First Term Judiciary; Picking Judges in the Minefield of Obstructionism," *Judicature*, vol. 97, July-August 2013, pp.41, 43. (Hereinafter cited as Goldman et al., "Obama's First Term Judiciary.")

[53] For a more detailed discussion of the selection process for circuit court nominations, see CRS Report RL34405, *Role of Home State Senators in the Selection of Lower Federal Court Judges*, by Barry J. McMillion and Denis Steven Rutkus (specifically, report section "Lesser Role for Senators When Recommending Circuit Court Candidates").

[54] There is also a 12th geographically based circuit court not encompassing any states, the U.S. Court of Appeals for the District of Columbia Circuit. Not geographically based is a 13th circuit court, the U.S. Court of Appeals for the Federal Circuit, a court that is headquartered in Washington, D.C. and has nationwide jurisdiction.

[55] See CRS Report RS22510, *"State Representation" in Appointments to Federal Circuit Courts*, by R. Sam Garrett; also, Kevin M. Scott and R. Sam Garrett, "Assessing Changes in State Representation on the U.S. Courts of Appeals," *Presidential Studies Quarterly*, vol. 41, no. 4 (December 2011), pp. 777-792.

[56] Cassandra Butts, Office of the White House counsel, Deputy Counsel to the President, telephone conversation with one of CRS authors, May 13, 2009. By early April 2010, CRS learned from another Administration source that of 18 persons nominated by that point to circuit judgeships, President Obama had selected 12 who were not candidates recommended by home state Senators. CRS Report RL34405, *Role of Home State Senators in the Selection of Lower Federal Court Judges*, by Barry J. McMillion and Denis Steven Rutkus, *Role of Home State Senators in the Selection of Lower Federal Court Judges*, by Barry J. McMillion and Denis Steven Rutkus (under heading "Lesser Role Well Established by Custom").

[57] Goldman, in *Encyclopedia of American Judicial System*, p. 589.

[58] See Goldman et al., "Obama's First Term Judiciary," observing, at p. 15, that in "the name generation and 'political' phases of the selection process, it remains the case, as it has in past administrations, that interactions with senators are handled almost exclusively by the counsel's office.... "

[59] The discussion under this heading draws largely from CRS Report RL34405, *Role of Home State Senators in the Selection of Lower Federal Court Judges*, by Barry J. McMillion and Denis Steven Rutkus (specifically, report section "Administration Entities and Their Roles"). For additional description of the contemporary pre-nomination selection process, see "Contemporary Practice," in Mitchel A. Sollenberger, *Judicial Appointments and Democratic Controls* (Durham, NC: Carolina Academic Press, 2011), pp. 52-68 (hereinafter cited as Sollenberger, Judicial Appointments), and Sheldon Goldman et al., "Obama's First Tem Judiciary," pp. 14-16 (under heading "Judicial Selection within the Obama Administration").

[60] "FBI review of judicial candidates has been a routine part of the pre-nomination process since Richard Nixon's presidency, but the practice can be traced back to at least the Herbert Hoover administration when Attorney General William Mitchell ordered investigations on the qualifications of applicants for judicial positions." Sollenberger, *Judicial Appointments*, p. 80.

[61] The 15 consist of two committee members representing the Ninth judicial circuit, one from each of the other federal judicial circuits, and the committee chair.

[62] In 2009, the Obama Administration reinstituted the White House practice, discontinued by the previous Administration of George W. Bush, of informing the ABA committee of judicial candidates under consideration and seeking the committee's evaluation of these candidates before making nomination decisions. Bringing the ABA committee investigation back into the pre-nomination stage, one scholar noted, injected into that stage an "additional 30 to 45 days typically consumed" by an ABA committee investigation of a nominee. Russell Wheeler, "Judicial Nominations in the First 14 Months of the Obama and Bush Administrations," *Governance Studies at Brookings*, April 7, 2010, at http://www.brookings.edu/~/media/research/files/papers/2010/4/ 07%20judicial%20nominations%20wheeler/0407_judicial_nominations_wheeler.pdf.

[63] The ABA committee's explanation of its role and the standards and procedures it uses in rating candidates for lower federal court judgeships is presented in the booklet *American Bar Association Standing Committee on the Federal Judiciary; What It Is and How It Works*, at http://www.americanbar.org/content/dam/aba/migrated/scfedjud/ federal_judiciary09.authcheckdam.pdf. (Hereinafter cited as *ABA Standing Committee; What It Is*).

[64] *ABA Standing Committee; What It Is*, p. 1.

[65] "In addition, interviews may be conducted of law school professors and deans; legal services and public interest lawyers; representatives of professional legal organizations; and community leaders and others who have information concerning the prospective nominee's professional qualifications." Ibid., p. 4.

[66] Ibid., pp. 5-6.

[67] When the committee vote is not unanimous, it is noted which rating received a majority of the committee's votes and which rating received a minority, as well as whether the majority and minority votes were or were not "substantial." Ibid., p. 6.

[68] If the informal report finds the candidate "not qualified," the White House may ask the chair of the ABA committee to appoint another evaluator to conduct a second review of the

candidate's professional qualifications. Ultimately, formal reports of both the first and second evaluator will be sent to the full committee for its review. Ibid., pp. 6-7.

[69] "In instances where a nominee has been rated 'Not Qualified' by the Committee and a hearing on the nomination is scheduled by the Senate Judiciary Committee at which the Committee is asked to testify, a written statement is prepared and submitted to the Senate Judiciary Committee explaining the reasons for the Committee's rating." Ibid., p. 8.

[70] For instance, a November 22, 2011, newspaper article reported that, in its pre-nomination evaluation of judicial candidates for the Obama Administration, the ABA committee had "secretly declared a significant number of President Obama's potential judicial nominees 'not qualified.'" As a result, the President, as of that point in his presidency, had "chosen not to nominate any person the bar association deemed unqualified." Charlie Savage, "Ratings Shrink President's List for Judgeships," *The New York Times*, November 22, 2011, at http;//www.nytimes.com.

[71] See, for example, Harvey Berkman, "ABA's 'Unqualified' Judges Doing Well," *The National Law Journal*, vol. 19, January 13, 1997, pp. A1, A20.

[72] See Sheldon Goldman et al., "Obama's First Term Judiciary; Picking Judges in the Minefield of Obstructionism," *Judicature*, vol. 97, July-August 2013, pp. 7-47.

[73] Also interviewed were "interest group representatives from groups ranging from very liberal to very conservative." Ibid., p. 7.

[74] Ibid., pp. 14-15.

[75] Goldman et al., however, noted that the selection of district court nominees was "historically tied more closely to home state Senators than circuit nominees." Ibid., p. 15.

[76] However, the scholars noted, unlike "virtually all cases of district court vetting" (where detailed vetting concentrated on only one person), sometimes more than one person would be thoroughly vetted for a circuit court vacancy. Ibid.

[77] The nomination is referred to the Judiciary Committee in conformance with two Senate rules—specifically Rule XXXI, which provides that nominations shall be referred to appropriate committees "unless otherwise ordered." and Rule XXV, paragraph 2(m), which outlines the jurisdiction of the Judiciary committee. See CRS Report RL31980, *Senate Consideration of Presidential Nominations: Committee and Floor Procedure*, by Elizabeth Rybicki (under heading "Receipt and Referral").

[78] As discussed later in this report, Senate rules permit the Senate to discharge the Judiciary Committee from a nomination by unanimous consent or by motion or resolution. CRS, however, in researching the processing of lower court nominations dating back to the early 1940s, has found no instances of the Judiciary Committee being discharged of a circuit or district court nomination. The Senate as well, by unanimous consent, could consider a circuit or district court nomination without first referring it to the Judiciary Committee. From the present day dating back to the early 1940s, however, CRS research has found only three instances of this occurring, all more than a half century ago. Specifically, on July 8, 1943, two district court nominations were by unanimous consent considered and then confirmed by the Senate without referral to the Judiciary Committee. U.S. Congress, Senate, *Journal of the Executive Proceedings of the Senate*, vol. 85, 78th Cong., 1943 (Washington: GPO, 1944), pp. 440, 450. In the most recent instance, a district court nomination made by President John F. Kennedy on August 2, 1961 was, by unanimous consent, confirmed the same day without reference to the Judiciary Committee. See Associated Press, "Senate Votes New Judge in Few Hours," *The Washington Post, Times Herald*, August 3, 1961, p. A2; also, Sen. Mike Mansfield, "Executive Session; U.S. District Judge," *Congressional Record*, vol. 107 (August 2, 1961), pp. 14432-14433..

[79] Specifically, in recent years, the Judiciary Committee's "Questionnaire for Judicial Nominees" has asked each circuit and district court nominee, among other things, for

- a complete employment record;
- a list of all professional, business, fraternal, scholarly, civic, charitable, or organizations in which the nominee had been a member since graduation from law school;
- a list and copies of all his or her published writings and public statements, "including material published only on the Internet";
- any judicial offices held and, if ever a judge, "the 10 most significant cases over which you presided,"
- citations for all opinions the nominee had written, and citations to all cases in which the nominee had been a panel member but did not write an opinion;
- a list of any cases in which a litigant or party had requested that the nominee recuse himself or herself as a judge due to an asserted conflict of interest, along with the reason for recusing or declining to recuse;
- identification of any public offices held, unsuccessful candidacies for elective office, or role played in a political campaign;
- a description of the 10 "most significant litigated matters which you personally handled, whether or not you were the attorney of record";
- a list of any clients for whom the nominee performed lobbying activities, with a description of the lobbying activities performed;
- teaching experience, including titles of courses and subject matter of courses taught;
- the sources, amounts and dates of all anticipated deferred income and future benefits;
- the sources and amounts of all income received during the calendar year preceding nomination and for the current calendar year;
- completion of an attached financial net worth statement in detail;
- "potential conflicts of interest when you first assumed the position to which you have been nominated";
- a description of instances and amount of time devoted in the past "to serving the disadvantaged"; and
- a description of his or her experience in the "entire judicial selection process, from beginning to end," including the interviews in which he or she participated (any interviews, for example, with home state Senators, or with White House Counsel's Office or Department of Justice staff).

[80] The Judiciary Committee's website provides online access to the completed public portions of the "Questionnaire for Judicial Nominees" for each circuit and district court nominee nominated in the current 113th Congress, at http://www.judiciary.senate.gov/nominations/judicial. The completed public portions of the questionnaires for judicial nominees in previous Congresses can be found (if the nominees received a committee hearing), in the applicable confirmation hearing documents of the Judiciary Committee published by the Government Printing Office.

[81] See Mitchel A. Sollenberger, *Judicial Appointments and Democratic Controls* (Durham, NC: Carolina Academic Press, 2011), pp. 222-223, for a blank copy of the confidential portion of the Judiciary Committee's "Questionnaire for Judicial Nominees." (Hereinafter cited as Sollenberger, *Judicial Appointments.*)

[82] Ibid., p. 107.

[83] On a few occasions, the scholar noted, a nominee's omissions of relevant information in the committee's questionnaire, when brought to the committee's attention, have moved some committee members to question the nominee's competence or integrity and to oppose the nomination moving forward. Ibid., pp. 107-109.

[84] These reports were produced initially for the Administration as part of its pre-nomination evaluation of judicial candidates.

[85] Sollenberger, *Judicial Appointments*, p. 109,

[86] See earlier section of this report under heading "Senators' Involvement in Selection Process Reinforced by Judiciary Committee's Blue Slip Policy."

[87] Senate Judiciary Committee website, "Judicial Nominations, and Confirmations," at http://www.judiciary.senate.gov/ nominations/judicial.cfm. (accessed on Jan. 17, 2013). The committee website statement noted, however, that a Senator may return a blue slip that approves committee consideration of a judicial nomination without also endorsing the nominee. "It is important to note," the statement said, "that the return of a positive 'blue slip' is not a commitment by either home state Senator to support or oppose a pending nomination."

[88] See again "Blue Slip Policy of Senate Judiciary Committee" and "Should the Policy of the Judiciary Committee Allow a Home State Senator to Block Committee Consideration of a Judicial Nominee?" in CRS Report RL34405, *Role of Home State Senators in the Selection of Lower Federal Court Judges*, by Barry J. McMillion and Denis Steven Rutkus.

[89] The Judiciary Committee often will receive the ABA rating of the nominee within days of the President transmitting the nomination to the Senate. This will be typical if, as has been the case in most, if not in all, recent presidential administrations, the judicial candidate has undergone ABA committee evaluation prior to being nominated. If, however, as was the case during the presidency of George W. Bush, the ABA committee were excluded from the Administration's pre-nomination investigative process, the ABA evaluation would be conducted after President selected the nominee. In such a case, the Judiciary Committee, after receipt of the nomination, might have to wait six or more weeks to receive an ABA rating, depending on the time needed by the ABA committee to complete its evaluation of the nominee.

[90] A majority in favor of a particular rating category will be identified as a "substantial majority" if 10 to 13 of the committee's 15 members voted for it, or as a "majority" if 8 to 9 members voted for it. (The chair, as the 15th member, would not vote on the rating except in the rare instance of a tie vote among committee members.)

[91] Background information provided to CRS by staff of Senate Judiciary Committee.

[92] The ABA committee's booklet about itself explains that the written statement is submitted to the Judiciary Committee 48 hours in advance of the nominee's scheduled confirmation hearing if the ABA committee "has at least seven days' advance notice of the hearing and is assured that the statement will not be disseminated publicly until the day of the hearing. Otherwise, the Committee submits its written statement 24 hours in advance of the nominee's confirmation hearing." *ABA Standing Committee; What It Is,* p. 8.

[93] For data related to the average and median wait time from nomination to committee hearing (as well for other stages of the confirmation process), see CRS Report R43369, *U.S. Circuit and District Court Nominations During President Obama's First Five Years: Comparative Analysis With Recent Presidents*, by Barry J. McMillion; see also CRS Report R43058, *President Obama's First-Term U.S. Circuit and District Court Nominations: An Analysis and Comparison with Presidents Since Reagan*, by Barry J. McMillion.

[94] Rule II.1 of "Rules of Procedure United States Senate Committee on the Judiciary," at http://www.judiciary.senate.gov/about/rules.

[95] See, for example, the April 13, 2011 confirmation hearing on the circuit court nomination of Henry F. Floyd to the U.S. Court of Appeals for the Fourth Circuit, who was presented to the Judiciary Committee by Representative James E. Clyburn of South Carolina as well as by Senator Lindsey Graham of South Carolina. U.S. Congress, Senate Committee on the Judiciary, *Confirmation Hearings on Federal Appointments*, Hearings, 112th Cong., 1st sess., April 13, 2011, S. Hrg. 112-72, Pt. 2 (Washington: GPO, 2012), pp. 6-7, 11-12.

[96] American Constitution Society et al., *The Path to the Federal Bench*, May 11, 2011, pp. 16-17, at http://napaba.org/ uploads/napaba/path_to_federal_bench-053111.pdf. (Hereinafter cited as American Constitution Society, *Path to Federal Bench*.) This 30-page pamphlet, in its introduction (at p. 1), stated it was "intended to serve as a guide for law students and lawyers early in their careers who are interested in pursuing an Article III federal judgeship in the future."

[97] Sollenberger, *Judicial Appointments*, p.120, commenting, also at p. 120, that most such hearings have a "pro forma quality" which "produces little public attention."

[98] American Constitution Society, *Path to Federal Bench*, p. 16.

[99] Rule III.2 of "Rules of Procedure United States Senate Committee on the Judiciary," at http://www.judiciary.senate.gov/about/rules.

[100] Sollenberger, *Judicial Appointments*, p. 118, commenting that "the hearing stage ... provides an opportunity for the public to see the individuals who may eventually sit on the federal bench. In addition, a hearing is often the only time judicial nominees are able to publicly address charges made against them and explain their approach to deciding cases."

[101] All of the aforementioned kinds of written statements will be included in the Judiciary Committee's published hearings document, along with the transcripts of the proceedings of the confirmation hearings themselves.

[102] Attesting to this practical requirement, the Judiciary Committee's website has stated that "After the completion of any follow-up questions, a nomination can then be listed for Committee consideration during an Executive Business Meeting." Senate Judiciary Committee website, "Judicial Nominations, and Confirmations," at http://www.judiciary.senate.gov/nominations/judicial.cfm. (accessed on Jan. 17, 2013).

[103] This unofficial hearing requirement for circuit and district court nominees is to be distinguished from the Judiciary Committee's practice with regard to nominations for U.S. Marshal and U.S. Attorney positions, which the committee almost invariably reports to the Senate without the need first for confirmation hearings.

[104] See, for example, archived CRS Report RL33839, *Returns and Resubmissions of Nominees to the U.S. Courts of Appeals and District Courts, 1977-2006*. (Copy available from author.)

[105] Advance public notice of the meeting and its agenda are posted on the Judiciary Committee's website, at http://www.judiciary.senate.gov/, as well as printed in the Daily Digest of the *Congressional Record*, under the Digest heading "Congressional Program Ahead."

[106] Rule III.1 of "Rules of Procedure United States Senate Committee on the Judiciary," at http://www.judiciary.senate.gov/about/rules. This is also a requirement in Senate Rules (Rule XVI, paragraph 7). See also CRS Report RS22952, *Proxy Voting and Polling in Senate Committee*, by Christopher M. Davis.

[107] The governing rule of the Judiciary Committee in this case provides that "At the request of any member, or by action of the Chairman, a bill, matter, or nomination on the agenda of the Committee may be held over until the next meeting of the Committee or for one week,

whichever occurs later." Rule I.3 of "Rules of Procedure United States Senate Committee on the Judiciary," at http://www.judiciary.senate.gov/about/rules.

[108] The most recent example of the Judiciary Committee voting to report a judicial nomination other than favorably occurred on May 1, 2003. The committee that day approved, by a 10-9 roll call vote, a motion to report without recommendation the nomination of J. Leon Holmes to the U.S. District Court for the Eastern District of Arkansas. Subsequently, on July 6, 2004, the Senate confirmed the nomination by a 51-46 vote. For discussion of this and earlier instances of lower court nominations reported by the Judiciary Committee other than favorably, see CRS Report R40470, *U.S. Circuit and District Court Nominations: Senate Rejections and Committee Votes Other Than to Report Favorably, 1939-2013*, by Barry J. McMillion.

[109] According to CRS data, for example, during President Ronald Reagan's first term, a total of 135 district court nominations were reported by the committee—none by roll call vote. In contrast, during President Barack Obama's first term, 169 district court nominations were reported, 24 (14.2%) by roll call vote.

[110] Usually, a judicial nominee rejected by the Judiciary Committee is not nominated again by the President. However, in some instances, a President has waited until a subsequent Congress to re-nominate, in the hope of a more favorable outcome in committee for the previously rejected nominee.

[111] Prior to adjournments or recesses of more than 30 days within a Congress, the Senate by unanimous consent may waive Paragraph 6 of Rule XXXI to have specific nominations not be returned to the President and instead remain pending in status quo, where they are, either in Senate committee or on the Senate's *Executive Calendar*. However, at the final adjournment of a Congress, all nominations still pending in committee or on the Senate floor fail of confirmation and are returned to the President, The nominees, nevertheless, may be re-nominated by the President in the next Congress, if the President chooses to exercise this option.

[112] Presidents have withdrawn judicial nominations under various circumstances. They have done so, for example, when the Judiciary Committee has voted against reporting the nomination, when there appeared little chance the committee would act on a nomination, or when the nominee has requested that his or her nomination be withdrawn.

[113] A CRS report explains that, under Senate Rule XVII, a Senator is allowed "to submit a motion or resolution to discharge a committee from consideration of a nomination. Such a motion or resolution would itself be subject to debate and potentially to a cloture process. The Senate does not, in current practice, employ a discharge procedure in relation to nominations, except in agreeing to unanimous consent to discharge a committee from consideration of a noncontroversial nomination." CRS Report R43331, *Majority Cloture for Nominations: Implications and the "Nuclear" Proceedings*, by Valerie Heitshusen (footnote to text under heading "Other Potential Effects on Presidential Nominations").

[114] CRS Report RL31980, *Senate Consideration of Presidential Nominations: Committee and Floor Procedure*, by Elizabeth Rybicki (under heading "Reporting").

[115] However, at least one notable, if unsuccessful, attempt to discharge the Judiciary Committee of judicial nominations occurred in 2003. In that episode, then-Majority Leader Bill Frist submitted four resolutions to discharge the Judiciary Committee from further consideration of four circuit court nominations. In each case, a Senator objected to immediate consideration of the resolution, and all four resolutions were placed on the *Executive Calendar*. No further action was taken on the resolutions to discharge, which under Senate rules would have been subject to debate and therefore subject to filibuster. See "Resolutions

Placed on the Executive Calendar," *Congressional Record*, vol. 149 (July 7, 2003), pp. 16949-16950.

[116] In addition, some executive branch nominations are listed along with judicial and other executive branch nominations even though they have never been referred to or reported by committee. For more information on these "privileged" nominations," see CRS Report R41872, *Presidential Appointments, the Senate's Confirmation Process, and Changes Made in the 112th Congress*, by Maeve P. Carey (under heading "Privileged Nominations, S. Res. 116").

[117] For a fuller description of this calendar, see CRS Report 98-438, *The Senate's Executive Calendar*, coordinated by Elizabeth Rybicki.

[118] A typical listing for a nomination on the *Executive Calendar*, in other words, simply reports that it has been reported by the committee in question, which is understood to mean (without information to the contrary) that the nomination has been reported favorably.

[119] The direct online link to the *Executive Calendar*, as of the cover date of this report, was: http://www.senate.gov/ legislative/LIS/executive_calendar/xcalv.pdf.

[120] "By precedent," a CRS report notes, "the motion to go into executive session to take up a specified nomination is not debatable. The nomination itself, however, is debatable." CRS Report RL31980, *Senate Consideration of Presidential Nominations: Committee and Floor Procedure*, by Elizabeth Rybicki (under heading "Taking Up a Nomination")..

[121] Ibid., elaborating that a "day for this purpose is a calendar day. In other words a nomination reported and placed on the Calendar on a Monday can be considered on Tuesday, even if it is the same legislative day."

[122] For an examination of the Senate's November 21, 2013, precedent (including an explanation of the procedural context in which the precedent was set and a discussion of the precedent's immediate and potential effects on the nominations process, see CRS Report R43331, *Majority Cloture for Nominations: Implications and the "Nuclear" Proceedings*, by Valerie Heitshusen.

[123] CRS research for typical examples of the use of the unanimous consent process to reach judicial confirmations, over a period of several decades, relied heavily on the tracking of this procedure in the Nominations database of Congress's Legislative Information System (accessed at http://www.congress.gov/nomis/). The database accounts for all nominations received in the Senate starting with the year 1987 in the 100th Congress.

[124] Technically, the support of 10 other Senators is necessary to order a roll call vote. See CRS Report RS20199, *Ordering a Roll Call Vote in the Senate*, coordinated by Elizabeth Rybicki.

[125] Senate experience in recent decades has included one instance in which a majority of the Senate voted against confirmation of a judicial nomination when the vote had been scheduled by unanimous consent. This occurred on October 5, 1999, when the Senate rejected the nomination of Ronnie L. White to be a U.S. district judge for the Eastern District of Missouri by a 45-54 vote. The Senate voted on the nomination pursuant to an October 4, 1999 unanimous consent agreement. This also was the last instance in which the Senate, in a confirmation vote, rejected a district or circuit court nomination. See CRS Report R40470, *U.S. Circuit and District Court Nominations: Senate Rejections and Committee Votes Other Than to Report Favorably, 1939-2013*, by Barry J. McMillion

[126] Unanimous consent also may occasionally be requested for the holding of a confirmation vote on a nomination even when objection to the request is expected and in fact subsequently is heard. For the Senator asking it, the UC request, despite the objection raised, serves as a

means to convey the Senator's view that the nomination in question is deserving of Senate approval.

[127] See "Unanimous Consent Requests—Executive Calendar," December 9, 2013, *Congressional Record*, daily edition, vol. 159, p. S8558; "Unanimous Consent Request—Executive Calendar," February 12, 2014, *Congressional Record*, daily edition, vol. 160, pp. S928, S939; and "Unanimous Consent Request—Executive Calendar," February 27, 2014, *Congressional Record*, daily edition, vol. 160, p. S1223. All four of these UC requests (with two separate requests made on February 12, 2014) were for the Senate to consider and confirm en bloc two or more district court nominations.

[128] CRS Report RL32878, *Cloture Attempts on Nominations: Data and Historical Development*, by Richard S. Beth.

[129] The difficulty in securing unanimous consent for an up-or-down vote on confirmation may be due to one or more Senators placing, through their party leaders, an anonymous "hold" on the nomination. Alternately, the leadership of one party, in the absence of a hold request, may, for other reasons, oppose a UC agreement setting a time certain for a Senate confirmation vote. For fuller discussion of "holds," see CRS Report R43563, *"Holds" in the Senate*, by Mark J. Oleszek.

[130] The motion for cloture, a CRS report notes, is the "only procedure by which the Senate can vote to place time limits on its consideration of a matter." CRS Report RL32878, *Cloture Attempts on Nominations: Data and Historical Development*, by Richard S. Beth (under heading "Cloture and the Consideration of Nominations").

[131] "In practice, the Senate agrees to unanimous consent requests (typically proposed by the majority leader or his designee) to proceed to executive session to take up a nomination on the Calendar; this practice is common since any Senator opposing the nomination knows that a majority could prevail on the motion to proceed if unanimous consent to proceed could not be secured." CRS Report R43331, *Majority Cloture for Nominations: Implications and the "Nuclear" Proceedings*, by Valerie Heitshusen.

[132] In recent years, cloture motions on most nominations have been filed by the majority leader. In some instances, however, when the party of the Senate minority and the President have been the same, cloture motions have been filed by the minority leder.

[133] CRS Report RL30360, *Filibusters and Cloture in the Senate*, by Richard S. Beth and Valerie Heitshusen. For fuller detail on the cloture process, see CRS Report RL30360, *Filibusters and Cloture in the Senate*, by Richard S. Beth and Valerie Heitshusen.

[134] CRS Report R42996, *Changes to Senate Procedures at the Start of the 113th Congress Affecting the Operation of Cloture (S.Res. 15 and S.Res. 16)*, by Elizabeth Rybicki

[135] CRS Report R43331, *Majority Cloture for Nominations: Implications and the "Nuclear" Proceedings*, by Valerie Heitshusen.

[136] See, for example, "Executive Session," *Congressional Record*, daily edition, vol. 160, February 24, 2014, p. S995; "Unanimous Consent Agreement—Executive Calendar," *Congressional Record,* daily edition, vol. 160, May 7, 2014, p. S2780; and "Unanimous Consent Agreement—Executive Calendar," *Congressional Record*, daily edition, vol. 160, May 20, p. S3161. .

[137] See, for example, "Orders for Tuesday, June 12, 2012," *Congressional Record*, daily edition, vol. 158, June 11, 2012, p. S3930.

[138] See, for example, "Nomination of Andrew David Horowitzz to be United States Circuit Judge for the Ninth Circuit," *Congressional Record*, daily edition, vol. 158, June 12, 2012, pp. S3931-S3949.

139 Sometimes, in having cloture motions filed on a series of nominations, the majority leader, either by unanimous consent or by motion, has the Senate proceed to executive session to consider the first nomination, immediately thereafter presenting a cloture motion. The leader then moves to proceed to legislative session, and after that motion is agreed to, the leader has the Senate proceed back to executive session to consider the second nomination, immediately thereafter presenting a cloture motion for that nomination, and so on. For an example of cloture motions being filed on a series of four district court nominations, see "Executive Session," February 12, 2014, *Congressional Record*, daily edition, vol. 160, p. S939-940.

In the absence of unanimous consent, filing cloture motions on a series of nominations could take time if 11 or more Senators were willing to demand roll call votes on several questions. A nomination must be under Senate floor consideration before cloture can be filed on it. The motion to go into executive session for the consideration of a specific nomination is not debatable; however, once in executive session, a motion to proceed to a nomination is debatable. As a result, the Senate would need to move out of and return to executive session each time it wished to take up a nomination on which cloture was considered necessary, in order to avoid having to obtain cloture twice: first on a motion to proceed directly from the consideration of one nomination to another nomination and second on the nomination itself. These two motions (to go out and to go in) could be subject to roll call votes (taking approximately 10-15 minutes each) if one-fifth of a quorum (11 Senators) demand the yeas and nays on each vote. Such roll calls are not typical, however. (For instance, they were not demanded in the February 12, 2014 example of multiple cloture motions being filed on district court nominations, cited at the start of this footnote.)

140 See CRS Report R42996, *Changes to Senate Procedures at the Start of the 113th Congress Affecting the Operation of Cloture (S.Res. 15 and S.Res. 16)*, by Elizabeth Rybicki.

141 See, for example, a UC time agreement concerning successive cloture votes on four district court nominations at "Executive Session," February 24, 2014, *Congressional Record*, daily edition, vol. 160, p. S995. The agreement provided that, if cloture were invoked on the first nomination, all post-cloture time be dispensed with, and that the Senate then vote on confirmation of the nomination; further, that following disposition of the first nomination, the Senate vote, successively for each of the next three nominations, first on cloture and then immediately on confirmation, with (in the case of each of these nominations) all post-cloture time being dispensed with. The UC agreement further expedited the processing of the nominations by providing that the confirmation votes on the second, third, and fourth nominations each be 10 minutes in length instead of 15 minutes otherwise allowed under Senate rules.

142 Multiple cloture attempts on the same lower court nomination have occurred infrequently. CRS has identified, over a period from 1968 to 2012, six circuit court nominations on which more two or more cloture attempts were made during a Congress, These specifically were one nomination in the 96th Congress, another in the 98th Congress, and four nominations in the 108th Congress. For one of the nominations in the 108th Congress, four cloture attempts were made (all unsuccessful); for another, seven cloture motions were made (all unsuccessful as well). No district court nominations, however, have been identified on which more than one cloture attempt was made. CRS Report RL32878, *Cloture Attempts on Nominations: Data and Historical Development*, by Richard S. Beth.

143 This, as discussed above, was when the Senate reinterpreted the application of its cloture rule, to require only a simple majority to invoke cloture on most nominations.

[144] For data on nominations subjected to cloture attempts from 1968 through 2012, see CRS Report RL32878, *Cloture Attempts on Nominations: Data and Historical Development*, by Richard S. Beth.

[145] Many post-November 21, 2013 confirmation votes on lower court nominations, however, have received more than three-fifths of the Senate voting in favor of confirmation, even though the voting in favor.

[146] For instance, the Senate may, by unanimous consent, agree to a 10-minute time limit for Senators to vote on a nomination instead of the usual minimum of 15 minutes allowed for roll call votes. See, for examples, "Nomination of Pamela L. Reeves to be United States District Judge for the Eastern District of Tennessee," *Congressional Record*, daily edition, vol. 160, March 5, 2014, p. S1302; also, "Unanimous Consent Agreement—Executive Calendar," *Congressional Record*, daily edition, vol.160, May 7, 2014, p. S2780;

[147] One Senator would need to request the roll call, and 10 would need to second the request. See CRS Report RS20199, *Ordering a Roll Call Vote in the Senate*, coordinated by Elizabeth Rybicki.

[148] According to CRS records, the five confirmed Reagan circuit court nominees who received roll call votes were James L. Buckley (DC Circuit; confirmed 84-11), Alex Kozinski (Ninth Circuit; 54-43), Daniel A. Manion (Seventh Circuit; 48-46), David B. Sentelle (DC Circuit; 87-0), and James H. Wilkinson, III (Fourth Circuit; 58-39). The H.W. Bush circuit nominee who received a roll call vote was Edward E. Carnes (Eleventh Circuit; 62-36).

[149] Sidney A. Fitzwater (N. TX), first nominated by President Reagan on October 29, 1985, was confirmed 52-43.

[150] Statistics in this paragraph were derived from CRS's internal judicial nominations database.

[151] Every circuit and district court confirmation vote by the Senate since November 21, 2013 has been by roll call not because this was required by the Senate's reinterpretation of Rule XXII (as it was not), but because, prior to each confirmation vote, a Senator present in the chamber has asked for the yeas and nays. The Senate last confirmed a district court nominee other than by roll call vote on November 4, 2013, when it confirmed Gregory Howard Woods by voice vote; it last confirmed a circuit court nominee other than by roll call vote on June 12, 2012, when it confirmed Andrew David Hurwitz by voice vote.

[152] For further discussion of the motion to reconsider, see CRS Report RL31980, *Senate Consideration of Presidential Nominations: Committee and Floor Procedure*, by Elizabeth Rybicki (under heading "Consideration and Disposition").

[153] Ibid.

[154] Discussion under this, as well as the following, heading was prepared with the benefit of informal reference materials and background information provided to CRS by the Office of Legislative Affairs, Administrative Office of the U.S. Courts.

[155] The exact wording of the statutory oath of office taken by U.S. circuit and district court judges is as follows:

I, [INSERT FEDERAL JUDGE'S NAME], do solemnly swear (or affirm) that I will administer justice without respect to persons, and do equal right to the poor and to the rich, and that I will faithfully and impartially discharge and perform all duties incumbent upon me as [INSERT OFFICE] under the Constitution and laws of the United States; and that I will support and defend the Constitution of the United States against all enemies, foreign and domestic; that I will bear true faith and allegiance to the same; that I take this obligation freely, without any mental reservation or purpose of evasion; and that I will well and faithfully discharge the duties of the office on which I am about to enter. So help me God.

[156] The requirements for determining seniority are specifically provided for in 28 U.S.C. 136(b), which states: "The chief judge shall have precedence and preside at any session which he attends. Other district judges shall have precedence and preside according to the seniority of their commissions. Judges whose commissions bear the same date shall have precedence according to seniority in age."

[157] Background information provided to CRS by the Office of Legislative Affairs, Administrative Office of the U.S. Courts.

[158] By contrast, it is rare, if not unheard-of, that a President re-nominates a person whose previous nomination was rejected or withdrawn.

[159] From 1939 to 2014, the Senate, in floor votes on whether to confirm, rejected one district court nomination in 1939, two in 1950, two more in 1951, and a sixth in 1999. See CRS Report R40470, *U.S. Circuit and District Court Nominations: Senate Rejections and Committee Votes Other Than to Report Favorably, 1939-2013*, by Barry J. McMillion. While the time span covered by CRS Report R40470 runs through 2013, there have, since then, been no additional Senate rejections of lower court nominations.

[160] A search of circuit and judicial nominations in the Nominations database of the Legislative Information System, spanning the years 1987 to the present, identifies a total of 24 circuit court nomination and 20 district court nominations withdrawn by Presidents during this period.

[161] The excepted nominations usually will be identified in the UC agreement by their Executive Calendar number or, if pending in committee, by the individual "PN" (presidential nomination) number assigned to them by the Senate executive clerk.

[162] Early in a new Congress, of course, re-nominations are much more likely to come from a President with two or four more years left in the presidential term than from an outgoing President, leaving office on January 20.

[163] For judicial nominees who have received a hearing in a previous Congress, committee practice varies—with a new hearing held for some nominees, but with an additional hearing for others waived.

In: Appointment Process for U.S. Circuit
Editor: Caleb Bowman
ISBN: 978-1-63485-587-7

Chapter 2

U.S. CIRCUIT AND DISTRICT COURT NOMINATIONS DURING PRESIDENT OBAMA'S FIRST SIX YEARS (2009-2014): COMPARATIVE ANALYSIS WITH RECENT PRESIDENTS*

Barry J. McMillion

SUMMARY

The selection and confirmation process for U.S. circuit and district court judges is of continuing interest to Congress. Recent Senate debates over judicial nominations have focused on issues such as the relative degree of success of President Barack Obama's nominees in gaining Senate confirmation compared with other recent Presidents, as well as the time from nomination to confirmation for nominees, and the relative prevalence of vacant judgeships compared to years past. This report addresses these issues, and others, by providing a statistical analysis of nominations to U.S. circuit and district court judgeships during the first six years of President Obama's time in office and that of his three most recent two-term predecessors, Presidents Reagan, Clinton and G.W. Bush. Some of the report's findings include the following:

---

* This is an edited, reformatted and augmented version of a Congressional Research Service publication R43931, prepared for Members and Committees of Congress, dated March 9, 2015.

- During his first six years in office, President Obama nominated 61 persons to U.S. circuit court judgeships. Of the 61, 53 were also confirmed during this same six-year period. The 53 confirmed Obama circuit court nominees represented the second-highest number of nominees confirmed during recent Presidents' first six years. President Clinton had the lowest number at 50. The percentage of circuit court nominees confirmed during President Obama's first six years, 86.9%, was also the second-highest, while the percentage confirmed during President G.W. Bush's, 75.0%, was the lowest. Of the four Presidents, President Reagan had both the greatest number (66) and percentage (97.1%) of circuit court nominees confirmed within the first six years of his presidency.
- Of the 270 persons nominated by President Obama to U.S. district court judgeships during his first six years, 250 (92.6%) were confirmed. Of the four recent two-term Presidents analyzed here, this was the greatest number and second-greatest percentage of district court nominees confirmed. Of the comparison group, President Reagan had the greatest percentage of district court nominees confirmed (97.4%), while President G.W. Bush had the lowest percentage confirmed (86.8%). President Clinton had, during his first six years, 90.2% of his district court nominees confirmed.
- The average number of days elapsed from nomination to confirmation for circuit court nominees confirmed during a President's first six years ranged from a low of 55.8 days during the Reagan presidency to a high of 366.7 days during the G.W. Bush presidency. The median number of days from nomination to confirmation for circuit court nominees confirmed during a President's first six years ranged from a low of 37.0 days (Reagan) to a high of 228.0 (Obama).
- The average number of days elapsed from nomination to confirmation for district court nominees confirmed during a President's first six years ranged from a low of 50.2 days during the Reagan presidency to a high of 219.4 days during the Obama presidency. The median number of days from nomination to confirmation for district court nominees confirmed during a President's first six years ranged from a low of 35.0 days (Reagan) to a high of 214.5 (Obama).
- The percentage of circuit court judgeships vacant on January 1 of President Obama's seventh year in office was less than the percentage of such judgeships vacant on January 1 of his sixth year in office (3.9% and 9.5%, respectively). The percentage of circuit court judgeships vacant at the beginning of President Obama's seventh year in office was less than the percentage vacant at the

beginning of the seventh year of the Reagan, Clinton, and G.W. Bush presidencies.

- The percentage of district court judgeships vacant on January 1 of President Obama's seventh year in office was less than the percentage of such judgeships vacant on January 1 of his sixth year in office (4.9% and 11.1%, respectively). The percentage of district court judgeships vacant at the beginning of President Obama's seventh year in office was less than the percentage vacant at the beginning of the seventh year of the Reagan, Clinton, and G.W. Bush presidencies.

INTRODUCTION

Article III, Section I, of the Constitution provides, in part, that the "judicial Power of the United States, shall be vested in one supreme Court, and in such inferior Courts as the Congress may from time to time ordain and establish." It further provides that Justices on the Supreme Court and judges on lower courts established by Congress under Article III have what effectively has come to mean life tenure, holding office "during good Behaviour."[1] Along with the Supreme Court, the courts that constitute the Article III courts in the federal system are the U.S. circuit courts of appeals, the U.S. district courts, and the U.S. Court of International Trade.[2]

This report concerns nominations made by President Obama and other recent Presidents to the U.S. circuit courts of appeals and the U.S. district courts.[3] Outside the report's scope are the occasional nominations that these Presidents made to the Supreme Court and the U.S. Court of International Trade.[4]

In recent Congresses, there has been ongoing interest in the process by which U.S. circuit and district court judges are nominated by the President and approved by the Senate. During Senate debates over judicial nominations, differing perspectives have been expressed about the relative degree of success of a President's nominees in gaining Senate confirmation, compared with the nominees of other recent Presidents.[5] Additionally, Senate debate has, at times, concerned whether a President's judicial nominees, relative to the nominees of other recent Presidents, had to wait longer before receiving consideration by the Senate Judiciary Committee or "up-or-down" floor votes on confirmation.[6] Of related concern to Congress has been increases in recent years in the number of vacant judgeships in the federal judiciary, the frequency with which vacant judgeships are considered "judicial emergencies," and the time it has taken to process nominations to fill judicial vacancies.[7]

Perhaps in response to some of the issues described above, the Senate, on November 21, 2013,

> reinterpreted the application of Senate Rule XXII to floor consideration of presidential nominations by overturning a ruling of the chair on appeal. For nominations other than to the Supreme Court, the new precedent lowered the vote threshold by which cloture can be invoked—from three-fifths of the Senate to a simple majority of those voting, thereby enabling a supportive majority to reach an 'up-or-down' vote on confirming a nomination.[8]

The reinterpretation of the application of Senate Rule XXII, hereinafter referred to as "the reinterpretation," was in effect from November 21, 2013, during the first session of the 113th Congress (near the end of President Obama's fifth calendar year in office) to the end of the second session of the 113th Congress (through President Obama's entire sixth calendar year in office). As of this writing, the reinterpretation continues to be in effect during the 114th Congress.

Purpose and Scope of Report

The purpose of this report is to provide an annual update of certain statistics related to the nomination and confirmation of lower federal court judges during the current presidency, with a focus on the aggregate or cumulative statistics related to the current President's first six years in office, as well as highlights from his most recent year in office (i.e., his sixth year).[9] Such statistics represent but one approach to analyzing the nomination and confirmation process for lower federal court nominees—other analyses, for example, might focus on nomination and confirmation statistics presented by Congress (rather than by presidency) or calendar year.[10]

Specifically, in light of continued Senate interest in the judicial selection and confirmation process, this report seeks to inform the ongoing debate in three ways: (1) by comparing the number and percentage of U.S. circuit and district court nominees who were confirmed during the first six years of the Reagan, Clinton, G.W. Bush, and Obama presidencies, as well as during just the sixth year of each presidency;[11] (2) by providing, for the same four

Presidents, a comparison of the time from nomination to confirmation for circuit and district court nominees approved by the Senate during each President's first six years; and (3) by comparing the percentage of circuit and district court judgeships vacant at the beginning of each President's sixth and seventh years in office as well as the percentage of such vacancies considered "judicial emergencies."[12]

In order to provide these statistics with some recent historical context, the report includes a comparative component (as described above) in which statistics during the current President's first six years are compared to the same statistics from other recent two-term presidencies. The report does not delve into analyses of issues more relevant to past presidencies but rather is intended to provide analysis and context related to the nomination and confirmation of the current President's judicial nominees.

This report does not analyze or take a position on the number or percentage of a President's judicial nominations that would be appropriate for the Senate to confirm, or on the average (and median) length of time that would be appropriate for, or needed by, the Senate to take final action on such nominations.[13]

OVERALL NUMBER AND PERCENTAGE OF CONFIRMED JUDICIAL NOMINEES

U.S. Circuit Court Nominees

Table 1 presents, during the first six years of a presidency for Presidents Reagan through Obama, (1) the total number of circuit court nominees; (2) the total number, and percentage, of circuit nominees confirmed by the end of a President's sixth year in office;[14] (3) the number, and percentage, confirmed after his sixth year; and (4) the number, and percentage, of circuit nominees never confirmed.[15]

Note that *Table 1* does not include individuals first nominated and then confirmed during a President's seventh or eighth year in office and, thus, does not reflect the total number or percentage of nominees confirmed during the full eight years of each presidency.

While Presidents sometimes have nominated particular individuals to a court more than once, *Table 1* counts such nominees only once (as does *Table*

2 below). In other words, neither table accounts for multiple nominations of the same individual to the same court.

Table 1 reveals that each President nominated between 61 and 68 individuals to circuit court judgeships during their first six years in office. Presidents Reagan and G.W. Bush nominated the greatest number of individuals (each nominating 68), while President Obama nominated the fewest number of individuals (61).

Table 1. U.S. Circuit Court Nominees: Number Nominated, Number Confirmed, Percentage Confirmed During First Six Years

		Number (Percent) Confirmed			
President	Number Nominated by End of 6th Year	By End of 6th Year	After 6th Year	Overall Number (Percent) Confirmed of All Those Nominated by End of 6th Year	Number (Percent) Never Confirmed
Reagan (1981-86)	68	66 (97.1%)	0 (0.0%)	66 (97.1%)	2 (2.9%)
Clinton (1993-98)	62	50 (80.6%)	4 (6.5%)	54 (87.1%)	8 (12.9%)
G.W. Bush (2001-06)	68	51 (75.0%)	4 (5.9%)	55 (80.9%)	13 (19.1%)
Obama (2009-14)	61	53 (86.9%)	TBD	TBD	TBD

Source: Internal CRS judicial nominations database.

Notes: This table shows the total number of individuals nominated for U.S. circuit court judgeships during a President's first six years in office, as well as the number and percentage of nominees confirmed during his first six years and after his sixth year. The table also shows the number and percentage of circuit court nominees who were nominated during a President's first six years who were never confirmed by the Senate. "TBD" is "to be determined" over the remaining two years of the Obama presidency.

President Reagan had the highest percentage of circuit court nominees confirmed by the end of his sixth year in office (97.1%)—all but two of the individuals nominated to circuit court judgeships from 1981 through 1986 were confirmed by the end of 1986. President G.W. Bush had the lowest percentage of circuit court nominees confirmed by the end of his sixth year in office (75.0% by the end of 2006), followed by Presidents Clinton (80.6% by the end of 1998) and Obama (with the second-highest percentage, 86.9%, by the end of 2014).

In terms of the number, rather than the percentage, of individuals approved by the Senate by the end of a President's sixth year in office, President Reagan had the greatest number confirmed (66) and President Clinton the fewest (50), followed by Presidents G.W. Bush (51) and Obama (with the second-highest, 53, by the end of his sixth year).

Of the eight circuit court nominees who were nominated during President Obama's first six years but not confirmed during that same period, two have, as of this writing, been renominated during the 114th Congress.[16] If these two nominees are confirmed, the number and percentage of nominees confirmed who were first nominated during President Obama's first six years, would increase to 55 and 90.2%, respectively.

Four circuit court nominees who were nominated during President G.W. Bush's first six years were eventually confirmed later in his presidency, raising the number and percentage of nominees confirmed who were first nominated during his first six years to 55 and 80.9%, respectively.

Four circuit court nominees who were nominated during President Clinton's first six years were eventually confirmed later in his presidency (i.e., during his seventh year or later), raising the number and percentage of nominees confirmed who were first nominated during his first six years to 54 and 87.1%, respectively.

Of those individuals nominated during the first six years of a presidency, President G.W. Bush had the highest number and percentage who were never confirmed (13 and 19.1%, respectively), followed by Presidents Clinton (8 and 12.9%) and Reagan (2 and 2.9%).[17]

U.S. District Court Nominees

Table 2 presents, during the first six years of the Reagan, Clinton, G.W. Bush, and Obama presidencies, (1) the total number of district court nominees; (2) the total number, and percentage, of district nominees confirmed by the end of each President's sixth year in office; (3) the number, and percentage, confirmed after his sixth year; and (4) the number, and percentage, of district nominees never confirmed.

Note that *Table 2* does not include individuals first nominated and then confirmed during a President's seventh or eighth year in office and, thus, does not reflect the total number or percentage of nominees confirmed during the full eight years of each presidency.

The table reveals that each President nominated between 230 and 275 individuals to district court judgeships during his first six years in office, with Presidents Clinton and Obama nominating the greatest number of individuals (275 and 270, respectively). President G.W. Bush nominated the fewest number of individuals during his first six years in office (234).

President Reagan had the highest percentage of district court nominees confirmed by the end of his sixth year in office (97.4%), while President G.W. Bush had the lowest percentage of nominees confirmed by the end of his sixth year (86.8%). President Clinton had 90.2% confirmed, while President Obama had the second-highest percentage (92.6%) confirmed during the first six years of his presidency.

In terms of the number, rather than the percentage, of individuals approved by the Senate by the end of a President's sixth year in office, President Obama had the greatest number confirmed (250) and President G.W. Bush the fewest (203).

Table 2. U.S. District Court Nominees: Number Nominated, Number Confirmed, Percentage Confirmed During First Six Years

		Number (Percent) Confirmed			
President	Number Nominated by End of 6th Year	By End of 6th Year	After 6th Year	Overall Number (Percent) Confirmed of All Those Nominated by End of 6th Year	Number (Percent) Never Confirmed
Reagan (1981-86)	230	224 (97.4%)	2 (0.9%)	226 (98.3%)	4 (1.7%)
Clinton (1993-98)	275	248 (90.2%)	4 (1.5%)	252 (91.6%)	23 (8.4%)
G.W. Bush (2001-06)	234	203 (86.8%)	24 (10.3%)	227 (97.0%)	7 (3.0%)
Obama (2009-14)	270	250 (92.6%)	TBD	TBD	TBD

Source: Internal CRS judicial nominations database.

Notes: This table shows the total number of individuals nominated for U.S. district court judgeships during a President's first six years in office, as well as the number and percentage of nominees confirmed during his first six years and after his sixth year. The table also shows the number and percentage of district court nominees who were nominated during a President's first six years who were never confirmed by the Senate. "TBD" is "to be determined" over the remaining two years of the Obama presidency.

Of the 20 district court nominees who were nominated during President Obama's first six years but not confirmed during that same period, 9 have, as of this writing, been renominated during the 114th Congress.[18] If these 9 nominees are confirmed, the number and percentage of nominees confirmed who were first nominated during President Obama's first six years would increase to 259 and 95.9%, respectively.

During the G.W. Bush presidency, 24 district court nominees who were nominated during his first six years were eventually confirmed later in his presidency (i.e., during his seventh year or later), raising the number and percentage of nominees confirmed who were first nominated during his first six years to 227 and 97.0%, respectively.

Four district court nominees who were nominated during President Clinton's first six years and two nominees nominated during President Reagan's first six years were later confirmed during each respective presidency, raising the number and percentage of nominees confirmed who were first nominated during each President's first six years to 252 (91.6%) and 226 (98.3%), respectively.

Of those individuals nominated during the first six years of a presidency, President Clinton had the highest number and percentage who were never confirmed (23 and 8.4%, respectively), followed by Presidents G.W. Bush (7 and 3.0%) and Reagan (4 and 1.7%).[19]

CONFIRMATION OF JUDICIAL NOMINEES DURING A PRESIDENT'S SIXTH YEAR

U.S. Circuit Court Nominees

Number Confirmed

There is variation across the four Presidents in the number of U.S. circuit and district court nominees confirmed solely during a President's sixth year in office. The number of circuit court nominees confirmed during a sixth year ranged from a high of 13 during the Clinton presidency to a low of 9 during the G.W. Bush presidency. President Obama had 12 circuit court nominees confirmed during his sixth year in office (the second-highest among the four Presidents), while President Reagan had 11 nominees confirmed.

The 12 circuit court nominees confirmed during President Obama's sixth year in office accounted for 22.6% of the total 53 circuit court nominees confirmed during his first six years in office. For Presidents G.W. Bush, Clinton and Reagan, the number of circuit court nominees confirmed during just the sixth year accounted for 17.6%, 26.0%, and 16.7%, respectively, of the total number of circuit court nominees confirmed during each President's first six years.

Comparison to Fifth Year

In general, at least during recent presidencies, the number of circuit court nominees confirmed during a President's sixth year in office is greater than the number confirmed during his fifth year. Of the four Presidents included in the comparison group, only President Reagan had a fewer number of circuit court nominees confirmed during his sixth year in office than during his fifth year (11 and 22, respectively). President Clinton had the greatest increase in the number confirmed between his fifth and sixth years (7 and 13, respectively).

The number of confirmed circuit court nominees also increased from the fifth to the sixth year during the G.W. Bush presidency (7 and 9, respectively), as well as during the Obama presidency (11 and 12, respectively).

U.S. District Court Nominees

Number Confirmed

For district court nominees, the number of nominees confirmed during a sixth year ranged from a high of 77 during the Obama presidency to a low of 21 during the G.W. Bush presidency. For Presidents Clinton and Reagan, 50 and 33 district court nominees were confirmed, respectively, during each of their sixth years in office.

The 77 district court nominees confirmed during President Obama's sixth year in office accounted for 30.8% of the total 250 district court nominees confirmed during his first six years in office. For Presidents G.W. Bush, Clinton and Reagan, the number of district court nominees confirmed during just the sixth year accounted for 10.3%, 20.2%, and 14.7%, respectively, of the total number of district court nominees confirmed during each President's first six years.

Comparison to Fifth Year

As with circuit court nominees, at least during recent presidencies, the number of district court nominees confirmed during a President's sixth year in office is greater than the number confirmed during his fifth year. Of the four

Presidents included in the comparison group, only President Reagan had a fewer number of district court nominees confirmed during his sixth year in office than during his fifth year (33 and 62, respectively). President Obama had the greatest increase in the number confirmed between his fifth and sixth years (32 and 77, respectively).

The number of confirmed circuit court nominees also increased from the fifth to the sixth year during the G.W. Bush presidency (14 and 21, respectively), as well as during the Clinton presidency (29 and 50, respectively).

The magnitude of the increase in the number of district court nominees confirmed by the Senate from the fifth to the sixth year of the Obama presidency is likely attributable, in part, to the interaction of the reinterpretation of the application of Rule XXII with a standing order that was in effect during the 113th Congress.

Under the standing order, if cloture was invoked on a district court nomination in accordance with Rule XXII of the Senate, post-cloture consideration was reduced from a maximum of 30 hours to 2 hours (circuit court nominations were not affected by the standing order). Consequently, the reduction of post-cloture consideration from 30 hours to 2 hours might have, in conjunction with lowering the vote threshold by which cloture could be invoked (from three-fifths of the Senate to a simple majority of those voting), made it possible for the Senate to confirm relatively more district court nominees than if both the reinterpretation and standing order were not in effect.

Many of the district court nominees confirmed by the Senate during President Obama's sixth year (i.e., the first full year in which the reinterpretation was in effect) had been nominated prior to the reinterpretation on November 21, 2013. Of the 77 nominees confirmed during his sixth year, 42 (54.5%) were first nominated prior to 2014 (i.e., prior to President Obama's sixth year in office.)[20]

LENGTH OF TIME FROM NOMINATION TO CONFIRMATION

The statistics and analysis presented in this section account only for those nominees who were confirmed by the Senate during a President's first six years (thus excluding from the analysis nominees who were never confirmed or who were later confirmed in a President's term, i.e., during his seventh year or later, and, for President Obama, those nominations for which final disposition has not yet been determined).[21]

Figure 1 tracks by President the average and median number of days from nomination to confirmation for all circuit and district court nominees confirmed during a President's first six years in office.[22] If a nominee was nominated more than once by a President during his first six years (and he or she was also confirmed within those six years), the first date he or she was nominated was used to calculate the days elapsed from nomination to confirmation.

U.S. Circuit Court Nominees

President G.W. Bush's circuit court nominees who were confirmed during his first six years waited, on average, the longest period of time from first nomination to confirmation (366.7 days). President Obama's nominees waited, on average, the second-longest period of time (258.0 days), followed by the circuit court nominees of Presidents Clinton (197.5 days) and Reagan (55.8 days).

In terms of the median number of days from nomination to confirmation, President Obama's circuit court nominees waited the longest period of time from nomination to confirmation (228 days), followed by President G.W. Bush's circuit nominees (216 days). The circuit court nominees who were confirmed during President Clinton's first six years had a median wait time of 113 days while President Reagan's circuit nominees had a median wait time of 37 days.

U.S. District Court Nominees

Figure 1 shows that President Obama's confirmed nominees waited, on average, 219.4 days from nomination to confirmation. President G.W. Bush's district court nominees waited, on average, 169.7 days. The district court nominees confirmed during President Clinton's first six years waited an average of 129.6 days while those confirmed during President Reagan's first six years waited 50.2 days.

The median waiting times from nomination to confirmation for district court nominees ranged from a high of 214.5 days during President Obama's first six years to a low of 35 days during President Reagan's first six years. For

Presidents Clinton and G.W. Bush, the median waiting times from nomination to confirmation for district court nominees were 99 and 133 days, respectively.

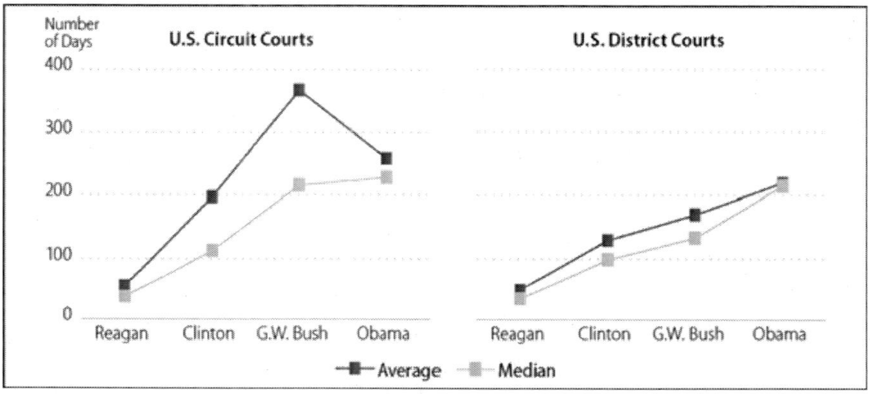

Source: Internal CRS judicial nominations database.

Notes: This figure shows the mean and median number of days from first nomination to confirmation for all U.S. circuit and district court nominees who were confirmed during a President's first six years in office.

Figure 1. U.S. Circuit and District Court Nominees: Mean and Median Number of Days from Nomination to Confirmation for Nominees Confirmed During First Six Years.

Length of Time from Nomination to Confirmation Prior to, and Following, the Reinterpretation of the Application of Rule XXII

Given that the reinterpretation occurred near the end of the fifth year of the Obama presidency,[23] judicial nominees confirmed during President Obama's six years in office fall into one of three groups depending on when they were first nominated and approved by the Senate.[24]

Specifically, 168 U.S. district court nominees confirmed during the first six years of the Obama presidency were both first nominated by President Obama and approved by the Senate *prior* to the reinterpretation (i.e., prior to November 21, 2013). The confirmation process for 40 additional nominees "straddled" the reinterpretation—i.e., they were first nominated prior to the reinterpretation but confirmed after the reinterpretation (i.e., after November 21, 2013). Another 42 nominees were first nominated, as well as confirmed, after the reinterpretation.

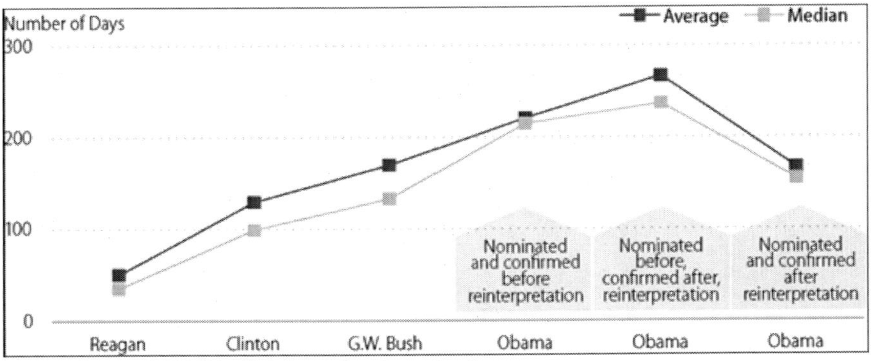

Source: Internal CRS judicial nominations database.

Notes: This figure shows the mean and median number of days from nomination to confirmation for six groups of U.S. district court nominees confirmed during the first six years of the (1) Reagan, (2) Clinton, and (3) G.W. Bush presidencies; (4) nominees confirmed during the Obama presidency who were first nominated and confirmed prior to the reinterpretation of the application of Rule XXII (i.e., prior to November 21, 2013); (5) nominees nominated during the Obama presidency prior to November 21, 2013, but confirmed after that date; and (6) nominees both nominated and confirmed after November 21, 2013.

Figure 2. U.S. District Court Nominees: Mean and Median Number of Days from Nomination to Confirmation for Six Groups of Nominees.

Among these three groups, as shown by *Figure 2*, U.S. district court nominees who were both nominated and confirmed following the reinterpretation, waited, in terms of the average and median, the fewest number of days from nomination to confirmation (167.0 and 154.5 days, respectively).

Compared to nominees confirmed during the three most recent two-term presidencies, the average number of days from nomination to confirmation for this group of nominees (167.0) was closest to the average waiting time for U.S. district court nominees approved by the Senate during the first six years of the G.W. Bush presidency (169.7)—this comparison is reflected in *Figure 2*.[25]

Additionally, as the figure shows, the average waiting time for this group of nominees remained longer than the average waiting times from nomination to confirmation for the nominees of Presidents Reagan and Clinton (50.2 and 129.6 days, respectively).

The median waiting time of this group of Obama nominees was also closest to the median waiting time of nominees approved by the Senate during the first six years of the G.W. Bush presidency (154.5 and 133 days, respectively). The median waiting time for this group of Obama nominees remained longer than the median waiting times from nomination to confirmation for the nominees of Presidents Reagan and Clinton (35.0 and 99.0 days, respectively).

The group of individuals first nominated before the reinterpretation but confirmed during the period following it, waited, both in terms of the average and median, the greatest number of days from nomination to confirmation (266.9 and 237.0 days, respectively). The group of individuals both nominated and confirmed prior to the reinterpretation waited, on average, 221.1 days from nomination to confirmation (with a median wait of 215 days).

As discussed above, a standing order in effect for the entire 113th Congress provided that, if cloture was invoked on a district court nomination in accordance with Rule XXII of the Senate, post-cloture consideration was reduced from a maximum of 30 hours to 2 hours (circuit court nominations were not affected by the standing order). Consequently, the reduction of post-cloture consideration from 30 hours to 2 hours might have, in conjunction with lowering the vote threshold by which cloture could be invoked in the first place (from three-fifths of the Senate to a simple majority of those voting), made the average and median waiting times to confirmation for district court nominees shorter than if just the reinterpretation had been in effect.

The focus of this section is on U.S. district court nominees. Of the U.S. circuit court nominees confirmed during President Obama's first six years, a relatively smaller number and percentage of them were first nominated, as well as confirmed, following the reinterpretation. Specifically, 4, or 7.5%, of 53 circuit court nominees fall into this group (compared with 42, or 16.8%, of 250 district court nominees confirmed during President Obama's first six years).

Of the comparable three groups of U.S. circuit court nominees, these 4 individuals waited the fewest number of days, in terms of the average and median, from nomination to confirmation— 149.5 and 151.5 days, respectively. In contrast, of the 10 individuals nominated to circuit court judgeships prior to the reinterpretation but confirmed during the period after it, the average and median number of days from nomination to confirmation was 305.3 and 241.0 days, respectively.

For the 39 individuals both nominated and confirmed prior to the reinterpretation, the comparable average and median number of days were 257.0 and 229.0, respectively.

U.S. Circuit and District Court Vacancies

Percentage of Judgeships Vacant on January 1 of Sixth and Seventh Years in Office

The percentage of vacant circuit and district court judgeships varies over the course of a presidency and is affected, in part, by the pace at which a President selects nominees for vacancies as well as the speed by which the Senate considers the President's nominees.[26]

Table 3 compares for the four Presidents: (1) the percentage of vacant U.S. circuit and district court judgeships on January 1 of a President's sixth year in office; (2) the percentage of vacant U.S. circuit and district court judgeships vacant on January 1 of a President's seventh year in office; and (3) the change in the percentage of vacant U.S. circuit and district court judgeships from January 1 of a President's sixth year to January 1 of his seventh year in office.[27]

Note that an increase (or decrease) in the percentage of vacant judgeships over a particular period of time is not solely a reflection of relatively fewer (or greater) number of nominations being confirmed by the Senate. It may be the case, for example, that the percentage of vacant judgeships increased during a particular period because a greater number of judges stepped down from active service than during the preceding period—thus, creating more vacancies.

U.S. Circuit Court Vacancies

Table 3 shows that the percentage of circuit court judgeships that were vacant at the beginning of a President's sixth year in office was greatest during the Clinton and Obama presidencies (12.8% and 9.5%, respectively) while, at the beginning of a President's seventh year in office, the percentage of circuit court judgeships that were vacant was greatest during the Clinton and G.W. Bush presidencies (9.5% and 8.9%, respectively).

The percentage of vacant circuit court judgeships at the beginning of President Obama's seventh year in office, 3.9%, was the lowest percentage of vacant judgeships on January 1 of any of the President's sixth or seventh years in office.

The table also shows that, of the four presidencies, the percentage of vacant circuit court judgeships decreased from the beginning of a President's sixth year to his seventh year during the Clinton and Obama presidencies (decreasing 3.3 and 5.6 percentage points, respectively). The percentage of vacant circuit court judgeships increased by 2.3 and 1.6 percentage points from the beginning of the sixth to the seventh years of the Reagan and G.W. Bush presidencies, respectively.

Table 3. Percentage of U.S. Circuit and District Judgeships Vacant on January 1 of Sixth and Seventh Years in Office

	Percent of U.S. Circuit Court Judgeships Vacant			Percent of U.S. District Court Judgeships Vacant		
	Jan. 1 of 6th			Jan. 1 of 6th		
President	Year	Jan. 1 of 7th Year	Change	Year	Jan. 1 of 7th Year	Change
Reagan	5.4	7.7	+2.3	7.7	7.2	-0.5
Clinton	12.8	9.5	-3.3	9.3	6.4	-2.9
G.W. Bush	7.3	8.9	+1.6	5.2	5.9	+0.7
Obama	9.5	3.9	-5.6	11.1	4.9	-6.2

Source: Internal CRS judicial vacancies database; CRS compilation of data provided by the Administrative Office of U.S. Courts.

Notes: This table shows the percentage of U.S. circuit and district court judgeships that were vacant on January 1 of a President's sixth and seventh years in office and the change for the respective type of judgeships between the two dates.

U.S. District Court Vacancies

As with circuit court vacancies, the percentage of vacant district court judgeships on January 1 of a President's sixth year in office was greatest during the Clinton and Obama presidencies (9.3% and 11.1%, respectively). On January 1 of a President's seventh year in office, the percentage of vacant district court judgeships was greatest during the Reagan and Clinton presidencies (7.2% and 6.4%, respectively).

The percentage of vacant district court judgeships at the beginning of President Obama's seventh year in office, 4.9%, was the lowest percentage of vacant judgeships on January 1 of any of the Presidents' sixth or seventh years in office.

From the beginning of a President's sixth to seventh year in office, the percentage of vacant district court judgeships declined during the Reagan, Clinton, and Obama presidencies (decreasing 0.5, 2.9, and 6.2 percentage points, respectively). The percentage of vacant district court judgeships increased slightly, however, from the sixth to seventh years during the G.W. Bush presidency (rising 0.7 percentage points).[28]

Percentage of Vacancies Deemed Judicial Emergencies on January 1 of Sixth and Seventh Years in Office

A vacancy is deemed a "judicial emergency" by the Judicial Conference of the United States if certain criteria are met regarding the number of case filings for that judgeship or court and, in some cases, the length of time a particular judicial vacancy has existed.[29] As with vacancies, generally, the percentage of vacant circuit and district court judgeships deemed judicial emergencies is affected by a combination of factors. A full accounting is beyond the scope of this report, but such factors include, in part, the pace at which a President selects nominees for vacancies as well as the speed by which the Senate considers the President's nominees.

For circuit court vacancies, a judicial emergency exists if adjusted case filings per appellate panel are in excess of 700 or, for any circuit court vacancy that is in existence for more than 18 months, where adjusted filings are between 500 to 700 per panel. For district court vacancies, a judicial emergency exists when a district court has weighted case filings in excess of 600 per judgeship; or a vacancy is in existence more than 18 months where weighted filings are between 430 to 600 per judgeship; or any district court with more than one authorized judgeship and only one active judge.[30]

Table 4 compares, for President Obama and two of his predecessors, (1) the percentage of circuit and district court vacancies considered judicial emergencies on January 1 of each President's sixth year in office; (2) the percentage of circuit and district court vacancies considered judicial emergencies on January 1 of each President's seventh year; and (3) the change in the percentage of judicial vacancies considered judicial emergencies from January 1 of a President's sixth to seventh year in office. Data on judicial emergencies is not available for the Reagan presidency; consequently, it is omitted from this part of the analysis.

U.S. Circuit Court Vacancies

Table 4 shows that the percentage of vacant circuit court judgeships considered judicial emergencies on January 1 of a President's sixth year in office was greatest during the G.W. Bush presidency (61.5%), followed by the Obama and Clinton presidencies (58.8% and 39.1%, respectively). The percentage of such vacancies considered judicial emergencies on January 1 of a President's seventh year in office was also greatest during the G.W. Bush presidency (81.2%). The percentage of circuit court vacancies considered judicial emergencies at the beginning of President Obama's and Clinton's seventh years was 42.9% and 64.7%, respectively.

Table 4. Percentage of Judicial Vacancies Deemed Judicial Emergencies by the Judicial Conference of the United States

	Percent of U.S. Circuit Court Vacancies			Percent of U.S. District Court Vacancies		
President	Jan. 1 of 6th Year	Jan. 1 of 7th Year	Change	Jan. 1 of 6th Year	Jan. 1 of 7th Year	Change
Clinton	39.1	64.7	+25.6	33.3	34.1	+0.8
G.W. Bush	61.5	81.2	+19.7	22.9	30.0	+7.1
Obama	58.8	42.9	-15.9	36.0	27.3	-8.7

Source: CRS compilation of data provided by the Administrative Office of U.S. Courts.

Notes: This table shows the percentage of judicial vacancies deemed judicial emergencies by the Judicial Conference of the United States on January 1 of a President's sixth and seventh years in office and the change for the respective type of judgeships between the two dates.

Of the three Presidents, President Obama is the only one for whom the percentage of vacant circuit court judgeships deemed judicial emergencies decreased from January 1 of his sixth year to January 1 of his seventh year (decreasing from 58.8% to 42.9%). For Presidents Clinton and G.W. Bush the percentage of vacant circuit court judgeships considered judicial emergencies increased by 25.6% and 19.7%, respectively.

U.S. District Court Vacancies

As shown by *Table 4*, the percentage of vacant district court judgeships considered judicial emergencies on January 1 of a President's sixth year in office was greatest during the Obama presidency (36.0%), followed by the Clinton and G.W. Bush presidencies (33.3% and 22.9%, respectively). The percentage of such vacancies considered judicial emergencies on January 1 of a President's seventh year in office was greatest during the Clinton presidency (34.1%). The percentage of district court vacancies considered judicial emergencies at the beginning of President G.W. Bush's and Obama's seventh years was 30.0% and 27.3%, respectively.

President Obama is the only one of the three Presidents for whom the percentage of vacant district court judgeships deemed judicial emergencies declined from January 1 of his sixth to seventh year in office (i.e., declining from 36.0% to 27.3%). For Presidents Clinton and G.W. Bush the percentage of vacant circuit court judgeships considered judicial emergencies increased (by 0.8 and 7.1 percentage points, respectively) from January 1 of each President's sixth to seventh year.

End Notes

[1] Pursuant to this constitutional language, Article III judges may hold office for as long as they live or until they voluntarily leave office. A President has no power to remove them from office. Article III judges, however, may be removed by Congress through the process of impeachment by the House and conviction by the Senate.

[2] The U.S. Court of International Trade is a nine-member court with nationwide jurisdiction over civil actions arising out of the customs and international trade laws of the United States.

[3] The U.S. courts of appeals take appeals from federal district court decisions and are also empowered to review the decisions of many administrative agencies. Altogether, 179 appellate court judgeships for 13 courts of appeals are currently authorized by law. In this report, nominations to U.S. courts of appeals judgeships are frequently referred to as "circuit court nominations." U.S. district courts are the federal trial courts of general jurisdiction. Altogether, 673 Article III U.S. district court judgeships are currently authorized by law.

[4] The scope of this report also does not include the relatively rare nominations made by a President to territorial district court judgeships, which were established by Congress pursuant to its authority to govern the territories under Article IV of the Constitution. The three U.S. territorial courts are located in Guam, the Northern Mariana Islands, and the U.S. Virgin Islands. Judges confirmed to these courts serve 10-year terms (rather than "during good Behaviour"). Like Article III courts, territorial courts hear cases arising out of federal law, their decisions may be appealed to a U.S. circuit court of appeals, and their judicial nominations are referred to the Senate Judiciary Committee.

[5] See, for example, floor remarks by Sen. Chuck Grassley in "Executive Session," Remarks in the Senate, Congressional Record, daily edition, March 4, 2014, pp. 1265-1266. See also floor remarks by Sen. Patrick Leahy in "Executive Session," Remarks in the Senate, Congressional Record, daily edition, September 9, 2013, p. S6285.

[6] See, for example, contrasting views on this and related issues in floor remarks by Senators Grassley and Leahy in "Executive Session," Remarks in the Senate, Congressional Record, daily edition, May 7, 2012, pp. S2909-2910 (Grassley) and pp. S2907-2908 (Leahy); and in "Nomination of George Levi Russell III, To Be United States District Judge for the District of Maryland," Remarks in the Senate, Congressional Record, daily edition, May 14, 2012, pp. S3120-3121 (Grassley) and pp. S3117-3119 (Leahy). These specific issues are not addressed in this report but data related to the average and median waiting times from nomination to committee hearing and from committee report to confirmation for recent Presidents' nominees are available from the author upon request.

[7] See, for example, Sen. Patrick J. Leahy, "Judicial Nominations in 2013," Remarks in the Senate, Congressional Record, daily edition, December 20, 2013, p. S9092. Concern over judicial vacancies has also been expressed by Chief Justice John G. Roberts, Jr., and by his predecessor, Chief Justice William Rehnquist. Chief Justice Roberts, noting that vacancies

are not evenly distributed across judicial districts, has stated that "a persistent problem has developed in the process of filling judicial vacancies.... This has created acute difficulties for some judicial districts. Sitting judges in those districts have been burdened with extraordinary caseloads." Chief Justice John G. Roberts, Jr., "2010 Year-End Report on the Federal Judiciary," January 2011, http://www.supremecourt.gov/publicinfo/year-end/2010yearendreport.pdf. Similarly, former Chief Justice Rehnquist argued that "[j]udicial vacancies can contribute to a backlog of cases, undue delays in civil cases, and stopgap measures to shift judicial personnel where they are most needed. Vacancies cannot remain at such high levels indefinitely without eroding the quality of justice that traditionally has been associated with the federal judiciary." Chief Justice William Rehnquist, "1997 Year-End Report on the Federal Judiciary," Third Branch, January 1998.

[8] CRS Report R43331, Majority Cloture for Nominations: Implications and the "Nuclear" Proceedings, by Valerie Heitshusen, pp. 1-2.

[9] A President's first six years in office is defined as the period of time between January 20, the date he assumed office during the first calendar year of his presidency, to December 31 of his sixth calendar year in office (rather than to January 19, which formally marks the end of his sixth full year in office but also falls during the seventh calendar year of his presidency). Operationalizing a President's tenure in office in this manner allows for the analysis to coincide more closely with dates for which congressional action on judicial nominations might occur (prior to the Senate adjourning sine die, i.e., prior to an adjournment that terminates an annual session of Congress).

[10] CRS is available upon request to provide analyses of nomination and confirmation data in ways other than how such data are presented in this report.

[11] Most of the statistics presented and discussed in this report were generated from an internal CRS judicial nominations database. Other data sources, however, are noted where appropriate. As mentioned above, statistics presented throughout the report account only for nominations made to U.S. circuit court and district court judgeships.

[12] For a discussion of the various factors that might help explain differences in judicial nominations statistics and judicial vacancies across presidencies, see CRS Report R43058, President Obama's First-Term U.S. Circuit and District Court Nominations: An Analysis and Comparison with Presidents Since Reagan, by Barry J. McMillion.

[13] The mean is equivalent to the arithmetic average ("mean" and "average" are used interchangeably throughout this report). The mean or average is calculated by adding a group of numbers and then dividing that value by how many numbers there are, while the median is the middle value for a particular set of numbers (i.e., half of the numbers are above the median and half of the numbers are below it). Although the average or mean is a more commonly used measure, the median is less affected by outliers or extreme cases (e.g., nominees for whom the time from nomination to confirmation was relatively much shorter or longer than it was for other nominees). Consequently, the median might be a better measure of central tendency.

[14] Not included as a confirmed nominee is any individual who received a recess appointment by the President and who was not subsequently confirmed by the Senate during that same President's first six years in office. So, for example, Charles W. Pickering, Sr., received a recess appointment by President G.W. Bush to the U.S. Court of Appeals for the Fifth Circuit on January 16, 2004. Mr. Pickering was not ultimately confirmed by the Senate and his judicial service ended on December 8, 2004. Consequently, he is not included as a confirmed circuit court nominee during the G.W. Bush presidency. For a discussion of

recess appointments, generally, see CRS Report RS21308, Recess Appointments: Frequently Asked Questions, by Henry B. Hogue.

[15] A judicial nomination may fail to receive Senate confirmation because (1) the full Senate votes against the nomination; (2) the President withdraws the nomination, either because the Senate Judiciary Committee (i) has voted against reporting it favorably, (ii) has made clear its intention not to act on the nomination, or (iii) because the nomination, even if reported, is likely to face substantial opposition on the Senate floor; (3) the nominee himself or herself has requested that the nomination be withdrawn; or (4) the Senate, without confirming or rejecting the nomination, returns the nomination to the President under Rule XXXI, paragraph 6 of the Standing Rules of the Senate after it has adjourned or been in recess for more than 30 days and the President does not subsequently resubmit the nomination to the Senate.

[16] The two nominees are Kara Farnandez Stoll, nominated to the Federal Circuit, and Luis F. Restrepo, nominated to the Third Circuit. The six nominees whose nominations were returned to the President (or withdrawn by him) and not ultimately resubmitted to the Senate include Robert N. Chatigny (nominated to the Second Circuit), Goodwin Liu (Ninth Circuit), Edward C. DuMont (Federal Circuit), Victoria F. Nourse (Seventh Circuit), Steve Six (Tenth Circuit), and Caitlin J. Halligan (D.C. Circuit).

[17] As indicated by Table 1, it remains to be determined, for U.S. circuit court nominees nominated during President Obama's first six years, the number and percentage of nominees who are approved by the Senate during the remainder of his presidency.

[18] The nine nominees are Alfred H. Bennett, George C. Hanks, Jr., and Jose R. Olvera, Jr., (each nominated to the Southern District of Texas), Jill N. Parrish (District of Utah), Dale A. Drozd (Eastern District of California), LaShann M. DeArcy Hall and Ann Donnelly (each to the Eastern District of New York), Roseann A. Ketchmark (Western District of Missouri), and Travis R. McDonough (Eastern District of Tennessee). The names of the 11 nominees whose nominations were unsuccessful (and whose nominations were not ultimately resubmitted to the Senate) are available from the author upon request.

[19] As indicated by Table 2, it remains to be determined, for U.S. district court nominees nominated during President Obama's first six years, the number and percentage of nominees who are approved by the Senate during the remainder of his presidency.

[20] This includes 10 nominees whose nominations were first made relatively late in the preceding fifth year of his presidency (i.e., nominations first made in October, November, or December of 2013). If those 10 late nominations are omitted, 32 (41.6%) district court nominees confirmed during President Obama's sixth year were first nominated during his fifth year or earlier in his presidency.

[21] Statistics related to specific stages of the confirmation process—from nomination to committee hearing and from committee report to confirmation—are available upon request from the author.

[22] As mentioned above, the "average" or "mean" is the arithmetic mean (both terms are used interchangeably throughout this report), while the "median" indicates the middle value for a particular set of numbers. In this case, the median is the middle value for the number of days from nomination to confirmation for a particular President's circuit or district court nominees. Although the average (also referred to as the mean) is the more commonly used measure, the median is less affected by outliers or extreme cases, e.g., nominees whose elapsed time from first nomination to confirmation was unusually long or short. Consequently, the median might be a better measure of central tendency.

[23] As such, the previous iteration of this report published in January 2014 did not include an analysis of how the reinterpretation of the application of Rule XXII might have affected the average and median waiting times from nomination to confirmation.

[24] For an analysis that is focused on nominees confirmed just during the 113th Congress (i.e., during President Obama's fifth and six years in office) see CRS Insight, U.S. District Court Nominees Confirmed During the 113th Congress: Time from Nomination to Confirmation Prior to, and Following, the Reinterpretation of the Application of Senate Rule XXII, by Barry J. McMillion.

[25] The average waiting time for the 42 nominees remained higher than the waiting times for district court nominees confirmed during the first six years of the Clinton and Reagan presidencies (which were 129.6 and 50.2 days, respectively).

[26] The percentage of circuit (or district) court judgeships that are vacant on any given date is calculated by dividing the number of circuit (or district) court vacancies that exist on a date by the number of authorized circuit (or district) court judgeships existing on the same date.

[27] Vacancies data provided by the Administrative Office of U.S. Courts at http://www.uscourts.gov/ JudgesAndJudgeships/JudicialVacancies/ArchiveOfJudicialVacancies.aspx.

[28] As reported previously by CRS, President Obama was the only White House occupant since at least President Reagan for whom the district court vacancy rate increased during a presidential first term unaccompanied by the creation of new district court judgeships. See CRS Report R43058, President Obama's First-Term U.S. Circuit and District Court Nominations: An Analysis and Comparison with Presidents Since Reagan, by Barry J. McMillion. As also discussed in this report, however, President Obama (of the Presidents included in the comparison group) had the lowest percentage of district court judgeships vacant on January 1 of his seventh year in office.

[29] The Judicial Conference of the United States is the principal policy making body concerned with the administration of the U.S. courts. The presiding officer of the Judicial Conference is the Chief Justice of the United States and membership of the Conference is comprised of the chief judge of each judicial circuit, the Chief Judge of the Court of International Trade, and a district judge from each regional judicial circuit.

[30] During the Clinton presidency, a judicial emergency was defined as any vacancy in existence for 18 months or longer.

In: Appointment Process for U.S. Circuit
Editor: Caleb Bowman
ISBN: 978-1-63485-587-7

Chapter 3

CLOTURE ATTEMPTS ON NOMINATIONS: DATA AND HISTORICAL DEVELOPMENT*

Richard S. Beth

SUMMARY

The motion for cloture is available in the Senate to limit debate on nominations, as on other matters. Cloture can, accordingly, be used to overcome a filibuster against a nomination. *Table 6* lists all nominations against which cloture has been moved, showing the outcome of the cloture attempt and the final disposition of the nomination. It would be erroneous, however, to treat this table as a list of filibusters on nominations. Filibusters can occur without cloture being attempted, and cloture can be attempted when no filibuster is evident. Often today, moreover, it appears that Senate leaders generally avoid bringing to the floor nominations on which a filibuster seems likely. In such cases there are no means by which to identify the merely threatened filibuster.

Until 1949, cloture could not be invoked on nominations. From then through 2012, cloture was sought on 122 nominations. On 46 of these nominations cloture was invoked, and on 49 others no cloture motion received a vote. All but one of these 95 nominations was confirmed. Only on the remaining 27 nominations did the Senate ultimately reject cloture; of these, 21 were not confirmed.

---

* This is an edited, reformatted and augmented version of a Congressional Research Service publication RL32878, prepared for Members and Committees of Congress, dated June 26, 2013.

Until 1968, cloture was moved on no nominations, and from then through 1978, it was moved on only two. Even thereafter, in no single Congress from the 96th through the 102nd (1979 through 1992) was cloture sought on more than three nominations, and in no Congress from the 104th through the 107th (1995 through 2002) was it sought on more than five. Between these last two periods, however, the 103rd Congress (1993-1994) foreshadowed a more recent pattern, with cloture action on 12 nominations. Most recently, in every Congress of the past decade (2003 through 2012) except the 110th, cloture has been attempted on at least 14 nominations. The same five Congresses that saw cloture action on 12 or more nominations are those in which the Senate minority was of the party opposite that of the President.

In all the Congresses or periods identified, no more than a quarter of nominations with cloture attempts failed of confirmation, except in the 108th Congress (2003-2004), when almost 80% of such nominations (mostly to judicial positions) were not confirmed. Prominent in this Congress were discussions of making cloture easier to get on nominations by changing Senate Rules through procedures not requiring a super-majority vote on cloture. In the 112th Congress, by contrast, cloture was moved on a record 33 nominations (again mostly to judicial positions), but on 23 of these nominations, no cloture vote ultimately occurred.

Overall, cloture has been sought on nominations to 67 executive and 55 judicial positions. Judicial nominations, however, predominated in the two Congresses just noted and before 2003, except in the 103rd Congress (1993-1994). In that Congress and the 111th (2009-2010), both at the beginning of a new presidential Administration, as well as in the 109th Congress (2005-2006), executive branch nominations predominated.

Few of the nominations on which cloture has been sought have been to positions at the highest levels of the government. These have included four nominations to the Supreme Court and seven to positions in the President's Cabinet (or ones often considered to be at the Cabinet level).

In recent years it has become increasingly common for Senators to seek cloture in order to limit chamber consideration of presidential nominations to positions in the executive and judicial branches of government. Cloture, which requires a super-majority vote, places time limits on consideration of a matter, and so may be employed as a means of overcoming filibusters. This report presents data on all nominations on which cloture motions have been offered (see *Table 6*). It also presents data on the outcomes of these attempts, the development over time of Senate practice in seeking cloture on nominations, and the positions in relation to which cloture has been offered. Before entering into these discussions, the report sketches some general features of cloture and considerations pertinent to interpreting its meaning.

CLOTURE AND THE CONSIDERATION OF NOMINATIONS

Senate Rules place no general limits on how long consideration of a nomination (or most other matters) may last. Owing to this lack of general time limits, opponents of a nomination may be able to use extended debate or other delaying actions to prevent a final vote from occurring. Although a voting majority of Senators may be prepared to vote for a nominee, the nomination cannot be confirmed as long as other Senators, presumably a voting minority, are able to prevent the vote from occurring. The use of debate and procedural actions for the purpose of preventing or delaying a vote is termed a filibuster.[1]

The only procedure by which the Senate can vote to place time limits on its consideration of a matter is the motion for cloture provided for in paragraph 2 of Senate Rule XXII. This motion, therefore, is the Senate's most usual means of attempting to overcome a filibuster. When the Senate adopts a motion for cloture on a matter, known as "invoking cloture," further consideration of the matter becomes subject to a time limit, and upon the expiration of that time a vote will occur.[2] For most matters, the time limit prescribed by the cloture rule is 30 hours, but under a standing order effective only for the 113th Congress (2013-2014), this 30-hour limit applies to post-cloture consideration of nominations only for the Supreme Court, Circuit Courts of Appeals, heads of Cabinet departments, and a small group of other positions often considered to be of "Cabinet rank." For most other nominations, the standing order limits consideration under cloture to eight hours, and for nominations to U.S. District Courts the post-cloture limit is two hours.[3]

By invoking cloture, the Senate may be able to ensure that a question will ultimately come to a vote, and can be decided by a voting majority. The Senate, however, can impose the constraints of cloture only by a super-majority vote. For most matters, including nominations, three-fifths of the full Senate (60 votes, if there is no more than one vacancy) is required to invoke cloture. As a result, even if a majority of Senators support a nomination, opponents may still be able to prevent a vote on it by defeating any attempt to invoke cloture, and continuing to extend consideration. The cloture rule permits supporters of a matter to move for cloture repeatedly, but any such motion still can be adopted only with a 60-vote majority. As a result, although any nomination can, itself, always be approved by a simple majority of Senators present and voting, the support of a super-majority may be required to limit consideration and enable the Senate to reach a vote.

CLOTURE MOTIONS DO NOT CORRESPOND WITH FILIBUSTERS

Although cloture affords the Senate a means for overcoming a filibuster, it is erroneous to assume that cases in which cloture is sought are always the same as those in which a filibuster occurs. Filibusters may occur without cloture being sought, and cloture may be sought when no filibuster is taking place. The reason is that cloture is sought by supporters of a matter, whereas filibusters are conducted by its opponents.

It is possible, as a result, that opponents of a matter may use debate and other procedural actions to delay a vote without supporters deciding to move for cloture. This situation appears not to be common today, but does seem to have occurred in relation to nominations in earlier times. Supporters may refrain from seeking cloture either because they think they lack the votes to obtain it, because they believe they can overcome any delaying actions and reach a vote without resorting to cloture, or because they hope to resolve the matter in dispute by some negotiated accommodation.

On the other hand, leaders of the majority party, or other supporters of a matter, may move for cloture even when opponents deny that they are conducting a filibuster, or at a point when no extended debate or delaying actions have actually occurred. They may do so in response to a threat or perceived threat of a filibuster, or simply in an effort to speed action. Under contemporary conditions, in particular, it has often appeared that Senate leaders attempt to avoid bringing to the floor matters, including legislation as well as nominations, on which they foresee a likelihood that filibusters will occur. These agenda choices may be motivated in part by a desire to avoid expending scarce floor time on matters that cannot be brought to a successful conclusion.

Compounding the potential for misunderstanding, in recent times observers have increasingly extended the use of the term "filibuster" to apply to situations in which opponents of a matter attempt in advance to discourage its consideration on the Senate floor. These situations are also sometimes described as "silent filibusters." They may arise, for example, when Senators inform their respective party floor leaders that they prefer the nomination (or other matter) not to receive floor consideration, an action that has become known as placing a "hold" on a matter. Although a "hold" has no formal procedural force under Senate Rules, it may represent an implicit threat to filibuster that may discourage the majority leader from bringing the matter to the floor.[4]

This newer sense of the term "filibuster" is sharply distinct from the historically better established usage described above, which refers to actions actually taken during floor consideration. Cloture motions cannot be used to identify "filibusters" in the sense of matters withheld from floor consideration, because action under the cloture rule is, itself, something that occurs only in the course of floor proceedings. Except by unanimous consent, indeed, cloture cannot even be moved except on a question already pending on the floor. On matters or which a filibuster is in prospect, as a result, the possibility of cloture can arise only if the leadership determines to bring the matter to the floor despite the possibility of filibuster, and at that point the previously "silent filibuster" either becomes an overt filibuster or fails to materialize.

In recent years, as well, when the possibility of a filibuster is foreseen, the Senate sometimes agrees by unanimous consent to consider a matter under time limits, but require 60 votes for its approval. Under this arrangement, which is occasionally used for nominations, the so-called "60-vote hurdle" or "60-vote threshold" preserves the possibility for a minority (if sufficiently large) to prevent approval, yet the time limit makes it unnecessary to offer any cloture motion. As a result, these cases of potential filibuster also are not identifiable from the presence of cloture motions.

If cloture cannot serve directly as a measure of filibusters, however, neither can any other specific procedural action. A filibuster is a matter of intent; any proceedings on the floor might constitute part of a filibuster if they are undertaken with the purpose of blocking or delaying a vote. Yet any of the procedural actions that might be used to delay or block a vote might also be used as part of a normal course of consideration leading without difficulty to a final decision. As a result, filibusters cannot simply be identified by explicit or uniform criteria, and there is no commonly accepted set of criteria for doing so. Instead, determining whether a filibuster is occurring in any specific case typically requires a degree of subjective judgment.

For all these reasons, it would be a misuse of the following data, which identify nominations on which cloture was sought, to treat them as identifying nominations subjected to filibuster. It would equally be a misinterpretation to assume that all nominations on which cloture was not sought were not filibustered (especially for periods before 1949, when, as discussed later, it first became possible to move cloture on nominations). This report provides data only on nominations on which cloture motions were offered. It is not to be taken as providing systematic data on nominations that were or were not filibustered. It would not be feasible to develop a list of measures filibustered unless a commonly accepted single standard for identifying what constitutes filibustering could first be established.[5] At most, the data presented here may be regarded as identifying some potentially likely cases in which a filibuster (by some appropriate definition) may have occurred.

FREQUENCY OF CLOTURE ATTEMPTS ON NOMINATIONS

The Senate first adopted a cloture rule (paragraph 2 of Rule XXII) in 1917. Until 1949, cloture could be moved only on legislative measures; nominations could not be subjected to cloture attempts.[6] From 1949 through 2012 (81st through 112th Congresses), cloture was sought on 122 nominations.[7] *Table 4*, following the text of this report, identifies the 122 nominations, the number of separate cloture motions filed on each, the ultimate outcome of the cloture attempt in each case, and the disposition of each nomination. As shown by the summary in *Table 1*, the Senate invoked cloture on 46 of the 122 nominations on which cloture was moved from 1949 through 2012. On another 48 nominations, cloture motions were offered, but never came to a vote, because the motions were withdrawn or vitiated by unanimous consent, or because they fell (that is, became moot before the cloture vote occurred). On the remaining 27 of the 122 nominations, the Senate voted against imposing cloture.[8]

Of the 122 nominations on which cloture was sought, 100 ultimately won confirmation. The 100 nominations confirmed include all 46 on which the Senate invoked cloture and all but one of the 49 on which no cloture vote occurred.[9] Even among the 27 nominations on which the Senate voted only against cloture, six were nevertheless able to achieve confirmation (completing the total of 100 nominations confirmed). The remaining 21 nominations on which the Senate ultimately rejected cloture failed of confirmation, in each case because, at some point after the final vote to reject cloture, the nomination was withdrawn from consideration, so that no final vote occurred.

Table 1. Cloture Attempts and Action on Nominations, 1949-2012

Cloture Action	Action on Nomination		Total
	Confirmed	Not confirmed	
Invoked	46	0	46
Withdrawn, Vitiated, or Fell[a]	48	1	49
Rejected	6	21	27
Total	100	22	122

Source: Compiled from data in Table 6.

[a]This group includes only nominations on which no cloture motion received a vote. "Withdrawn" and "vitiated" mean that the Senate disregarded the cloture motion, and took no further action on it. "Fell" means that the cloture motion received no vote because it became moot.

Overall, none of the 22 nominations that failed of confirmation following a cloture motion was rejected by the Senate on an "up-or-down" vote. This pattern is consistent with Senate action on nominations generally; in contemporary practice, nominations that reach a final vote are very seldom rejected.

Historical Development of Cloture Attempts on Nominations

The assertion is sometimes made that filibusters against nominations were infrequent until recent years. Little comprehensive knowledge, however, exists about such filibusters in earlier times. One reason is that until 1929, the Senate normally considered nominations in closed session. Until 1917, moreover, the Senate had no rule for bringing debate on any matter to a close, and even thereafter, the cloture rule did not apply to nominations until 1949. For any earlier years, accordingly, it would not be even possible to try to use cloture as a measure of filibustering on nominations.

Certainly, some historical accounts reference instances of lame duck sessions preceding a change in party control of the presidency in which the Senate generally declined to confirm nominations by the outgoing President. Even in these cases, however, it is not clear that the nominations often failed as a result of filibusters on the floor.

There is, nevertheless, some reason to think that in earlier periods, filibustering on nominations was, indeed, infrequent. It is not clear, however, that this condition prevailed chiefly because Senate practice discouraged filibustering in such cases. Instead, it appears that Presidents often may have submitted nominations only after prior consultation with Senators. There also seems reason to suppose that often, when any Senators strongly objected to a nomination, the Senate might decline to bring the matter to the floor in the first place. The custom of "Senatorial courtesy," under which the Senate would decline to consider a nomination to a position in the home state of a Senator who declared the nomination "personally obnoxious" to him, represented an instance of such practices.[10]

To the extent that these suppositions are well founded, it might be said, in effect, that during these earlier periods, obstacles to the confirmation of nominations manifested themselves more often in the form of what today might be called "silent filibusters" than through overt opposition during floor consideration. The prevalence of such situations, of course, could not be ascertained from the examination of floor proceedings.

Even after Senate rules began to permit the use of cloture on nominations in 1949, cloture was sought on none until 1968 (90th Congress), when a motion to proceed to consider the nomination of Supreme Court Associate Justice Abe Fortas to be Chief Justice was debated at length. After the Senate rejected cloture on the motion to proceed, 45-43, President Lyndon B. Johnson withdrew the nomination. In 1969 and 1970, the nominations of Clement F. Haynsworth and G. Harrold Carswell to the Supreme Court were defeated after lengthy debate, but no cloture motion was filed on either. When the Senate considered the nomination to the Supreme Court of William H. Rehnquist late in the 1971 session, however, cloture was quickly sought. Though the Senate did not invoke cloture (52-42), the nomination was subsequently confirmed.

Cloture was sought on no other nomination until 1980. That occurrence was the first in which cloture was sought on a nomination to an executive branch position, that of William G. Lubbers to be General Counsel of the National Labor Relations Board. Cloture was invoked, and the nomination was confirmed.

In the meantime, the majority required for invoking cloture on most matters, including nominations, had been changed in 1975 from two-thirds of Senators present and voting to three-fifths of the full membership of the Senate (60 votes, assuming no more than one vacancy).[11] This change in the rules generally meant that the threshold for invoking cloture was lowered: if all 100 Senators participated in the vote, the previous rule required the votes of 67 to invoke cloture; the new rule normally required 60 votes, regardless of how many Senators participated.

Table 2. Nominations on Which Cloture Was Moved and Rejected, by Time Period, 1949-2012

Congresses (years)	Nominations on Which Cloture Was:			
	Moved		Rejected	
	Number	Average per Congress	Number	Percentage of Moved
81st-89th (1949-1966)	0	0.0	0	—
90th-102nd (1967-1992)	12	0.9	2	17%
103rd (1993-1994)	12	12	3	25%
104th-107th (1995-2002)	11	2.8	2	18%
108th (2003-2004)	14	14	11	79%
109th (2005-2006)	18	18	2	11%
110th (2007-2008)	1	1	0	0%
111th (2009-2010)	21	21	2	10%
112th (2011-2012)	33	33	5	15%

Source: Compiled from data in Table 6.

Since 1980, as *Table 2* illustrates, the frequency with which nominations have been subjected to cloture attempts has continually tended to increase (a development that parallels a trend in the frequency of cloture motions overall). In this table (and *Table 3* below), data on each Congress in which cloture was moved on more than 10 nominations are set forth separately, but data for suitable groups of consecutive Congresses with less frequent cloture action on nominations are consolidated in a single row.

Not only do the data in *Table 2* manifest a generally rising trend, but the pattern displayed in Congresses beginning with the 108th (2003-2004) is sharply distinct from that of earlier ones. From the 90th through the 107th Congress (1967-2002), cloture was only once (103rd Congress, 1993-1994) sought on more than five nominations. In the five Congresses from the 108th through the 112th (2003-2012), by contrast, cloture has only once (110th Congress, 2007-2008) been sought on fewer than 14 nominations.

The 103rd, 107th, and 111th Congresses were each the first of a new presidential Administration, so that the number of nominations to be considered was presumably large. Nevertheless, the new level of nominations with cloture attempts that was reached in the 103rd Congress remained exceptional until the 108th Congress, but the pattern of activity from then on has increasingly come to make the 103rd Congress look like a forerunner of practices that have now become typical. It may also be pertinent, however, that the same five Congresses in which cloture has been sought on 12 or more nominations have also been the only five Congresses since 1987 in which the same political party both occupied the presidency and commanded a Senate majority.[12] This pattern suggests that highly controversial nominations may now be more likely to be brought to the Senate floor if it is the President's party that can set the agenda.

In the 108th Congress (2003-2004), the pattern of Senate action on nominations on which cloture was sought displayed several distinctive features. This was the Congress during which extensive contestation occurred over attempts to secure confirmation for a series of judicial nominations by President George W. Bush, and the prospect arose that an attempt would be made to change Senate rules for considering nominations through proceedings (known as the "nuclear" or "constitutional option") that would not require super-majority support.[13]

First, the maximum number of cloture motions offered on any single nomination was markedly higher in the 108th Congress than in any other. Only three times previously had as many as three cloture motions been offered on a single nomination,[14] and only twice subsequently have as many as two cloture motions been offered on the same nomination.[15] In the 108th Congress, by contrast, one nomination was subjected to seven cloture motions and another to four.[16] These events suggest the intensity with which supporters of these nominations were attempting to secure Senate votes thereon. The more recent pattern, by contrast, suggests that Senate leaders have become less willing to invest extensive floor time on attempts to secure confirmation for nominations that command insufficient support for cloture.

The Senate in the 108th Congress also rejected cloture with much greater frequency on nominations on which it was moved. In this Congress the Senate ultimately voted against cloture on more than three-quarters of such nominations, which suggests that opponents were persisting in contesting these nominations much more intensely than has otherwise been the case. In all other Congresses (or, when cloture was attempted on only a few nominations in each of several consecutive Congresses, as shown in *Table 2*, in the group of consecutive Congresses as a whole), the Senate ultimately voted against cloture on no more than one-quarter of the nominations in question. This finding echoes the observation offered earlier that only a few nominations have been blocked by failure to obtain cloture.

Table 3. Cloture Action on Judicial and Executive Nominations, by Time Period, 1967-2012

			Judicial				Executive	
Congresses and (years)	Total	Cloture Invoked	Cloture Withdrawn, Vitiated, or Fell[a]	Cloture Rejected	Total	Cloture Invoked	Cloture Withdrawn, Vitiated, or Fell[a]	Cloture Rejected
90th-102nd (1967-1992)	8	5	1	2	4	4	0	0
103rd (1993-1994)	2	1	1	0	10	3	4	3
104th-107th (1995-2002)	7	5	1	1	4	3	0	1
108th (2003-2004)	12	0	2	10	2	0	1	1
109th (2005-2006)	6	6	0	0	12	3	7	2
110th (2007-2008)	1	1	0	0	0	0	0	0
111th (2009-2010)	5	2	3	0	16	8	6	2
112th (2011-20112)	26	3	20	3	7	2	3	2
Total	67	23	28	16	55	23	21	11

Source: Compiled from data in Table 6.

[a] This column counts only nominations on which no cloture motion received a vote. "Withdrawn" and "vitiated" mean that the Senate disregarded the cloture motion, and took no further action on it. "Fell" means that the cloture motion received no vote because it became moot.

POSITIONS IN RELATION TO WHICH CLOTURE WAS SOUGHT

Over the full period during which cloture motions have been used on nominations, as shown by *Table 3*, cloture action has occurred on nominations to positions in the judiciary and in the executive branch in roughly comparable numbers. Until the 111th Congress, however, a majority of the nominations on which cloture was sought had been to positions on the federal bench. This circumstance perhaps reflected the Senate's traditional inclination to permit the President generally wide latitude in selecting officials to serve under him in executive branch positions.[17]

More generally, however, the relative emphasis on nominations to positions in the two branches has shifted sharply from one Congress to another. In both of the periods identified in *Table 3* that cover several consecutive Congresses, as well as in the 108th Congress (2003-2004) and the 112th Congress (2011-2012), nominations to judicial positions were the main focus of cloture action. In the

103rd (1993-1994), 109th (2005-2006), and 111th (2009-2010) Congresses, cloture motions on executive branch nominations were more prevalent. It is perhaps pertinent that the 103rd and 111th Congresses both included the period immediately following the inauguration of a new President, when presumably there were a large number of nominations to positions in the new Administration. By contrast, Congresses in which a greater number of judicial nominations were subjected to cloture motions all fell after the beginning of a new presidential Administration.

As already observed, the only period during which cloture attempts on either class of nominations were rejected far more often than they were either invoked or abandoned occurred in connection with the broad struggle over President George W. Bush's judicial nominations in the 108th Congress (2003-2004). Either cloture was invoked, or no vote occurred, in especially high proportions on executive branch nominations in the 109th (2005-2006) and 111th (2009-2010) Congresses. On an especially high proportion of judicial nominations on which cloture was attempted in the 112th Congress (2011-2012), no cloture votes ultimately occurred, suggesting that cloture might have been moved on many of these nominations in response to perceived threats of filibuster that did not materialize or, perhaps, that proved susceptible of negotiated resolution.

Few of the nominations on which cloture has been attempted have been to positions of the first rank in the federal government. Only four have been to the Supreme Court, as shown in *Table 4*, and only seven to the heads of Cabinet departments or other positions sometimes accorded Cabinet rank by the President, as shown in *Table 5*. In relation to offices at lower levels of the executive branch, it can be discerned from *Table 6* that cloture attempts have occurred particularly often on nominations to positions in the Department of State and the Department of Justice.

Table 4. Supreme Court Nominations with Cloture Attempts

Date	Nominee	Position
1968	Abe Fortas	Chief Justice
1971	William H. Rehnquist	Associate Justice
1986	William H. Rehnquist	Chief Justice
2006	Samuel L. Alito	Associate Justice

Source: Compiled from data in Table 6.

Table 5. "Cabinet Rank" Nominations with Cloture Attempts

Date	Nominee	Position[a]
1987	C. William Verity	Secretary of Commerce
2003	Michael O. Leavitt	Administrator, Environmental Protection Agency
2005	John R. Bolton	U.S. Representative to the United Nations
2005	Stephen L. Johnson	Administrator, Environmental Protection Agency
2005	Robert J. Portman	U.S. Trade Representative
2006	Dirk Kempthorne	Secretary of the Interior
2009	Hilda Solis	Secretary of Labor

Source: Compiled from data in Table 6.

[a] Includes heads of Cabinet departments and other positions that have sometimes been accorded Cabinet rank by the President.

Table 6. Nominations with Cloture Attempts

Congress and Year	Nominee	Position	Number of Cloture Attempts[a]	Final Outcome of Cloture Attempt[b]	Disposition of Nominationc
90th, 1968	Abe Fortas	Chief Justice	1	rejected, 45-43	withdrawn
92nd, 1971	William H. Rehnquist	Associate Justice	2	rejected, 52-42	confirmed, 68-26
96th, 1980	William A. Lubbers	General Counsel, National Labor Relations Board	3	invoked, 62-34	confirmed, 57-39
96th, 1980	Don Zimmerman	Member, National Labor Relations Board	3	invoked, 63-31	confirmed, 68-27
96th, 1980	Stephen G. Breyer	Circuit Judge	2	invoked, 68-28	confirmed, 80-11
98th, 1984	J. Harvie Wilkinson	Circuit Judge	2	invoked, 65-32	confirmed, 58-39
99th, 1986	Sidney A. Fitzwater	District Judge	1	invoked, 64-33	confirmed, 52-42
99th, 1986	Daniel A. Manion	Circuit Judge	1	withdrawn	confirmed, 48-46
99th, 1986	William H. Rehnquist	Chief Justice	1	invoked, 68-31	confirmed, 65-33
100th, 1987	Melissa Wells	Ambassador	1	invoked, 64-24	confirmed, 64-24
100th, 1987	C. William Verity	Secretary of Commerce	1	invoked, 85-8	confirmed, 84-11

Table 6. (Continued)

Congress and Year	Nominee	Position	Number of Cloture Attempts[a]	Final Outcome of Cloture Attempt[b]	Disposition of Nomination[c]
102nd, 1992	Edward Earl Carnes, Jr.	Circuit Judge	1	invoked, 66-30	confirmed, 62-36
103rd, 1993	Walter Dellinger	Assistant Attorney General	2	rejected, 59-39	confirmed, 65-34
103rd, 1993	Five nominations[d]	State Department	2	rejected, 58-42	confirmed, voice
103rd, 1993	Janet Napolitano	U.S. Attorney	1	invoked, 72-26	confirmed, voice
103rd, 1994	M. Larry Lawrence	Ambassador	1	fell	confirmed, 79-16
103rd, 1994	Rosemary Barkett	Circuit Judge	1	withdrawn	confirmed, 61-37
103rd, 1994	Sam Brown	Ambassador	3	rejected, 56-42	no final vote
103rd, 1994	Derek Shearer	Ambassador	2	invoked, 62-36	confirmed, 67-31
103rd, 1994	Ricki Tigert	Board Member and Chair, Federal Deposit Insurance Corporation[e]	2	invoked, 63-32	confirmed, 90-7
103rd, 1994	H. Lee Sarokin	Circuit Judge	1	invoked, 85-12	confirmed, 63-35
103rd, 1994	Buster Glosson	Air Force Lieutenant General (retired)	1	withdrawn	confirmed, 59-30
103rd, 1994	Claude Bolton, Jr.	Air Force Brigadier General	1	vitiated	confirmed, voice
103rd, 1994	Edward P. Barry, Jr.	Air Force Lieutenant General (retired)	1	vitiated	confirmed, voice
104th, 1995	Henry Foster	Surgeon General	2	rejected, 57-43	no final vote
105th, 1997	Joel I. Klein	Assistant Attorney General	1	invoked, 78-11	confirmed, 88-12
105th, 1998	David Satcher	Surgeon General	1	invoked, 75-23	confirmed, 63-35
106th, 1999	Brian Theadore Stewart	District Judge	1	rejected, 55-44	confirmed, 93-5
106th, 2000	Marsha L. Berzon	Circuit Judge	1	invoked, 86-13	confirmed, 64-34

Congress and Year	Nominee	Position	Number of Cloture Attempts[a]	Final Outcome of Cloture Attempt[b]	Disposition of Nominationc
106th, 2000	Richard A. Paez	Circuit Judge	1	invoked, 85-14	confirmed, 59-39
107th, 2002	Lavenski R. Smith	Circuit Judge	1	invoked, 94-3	confirmed, voice
107th, 2002	Richard R. Clifton	Circuit Judge	1	invoked, 97-1	confirmed, 98-0
107th, 2002	Richard H. Carmona	Surgeon General	1	invoked, 98-0	confirmed, voice
107th, 2002	Julia Smith Gibbons	Circuit Judge	1	invoked, 89-0	confirmed, 95-0
107th, 2002	Dennis W. Shedd	Circuit Judge	1	vitiated	confirmed, 55-44
108th, 2003	Victor J. Wolski	Judge, Court of Claims	1	vitiated	confirmed, 54-43
108th, 2003	Miguel A. Estrada	Circuit Judge	7	rejected, 55-43	withdrawn
108th, 2003	Michael O. Leavitt	Administrator, Environmental Protection Agency	1	withdrawn	confirmed, 88-8
108th, 2003	Charles W. Pickering, Sr.	Circuit Judge	1	rejected, 54-43	no final vote
108th, 2003	William H. Pryor, Jr.	Circuit Judge	2	rejected, 51-43	no final vote
108th, 2003	Priscilla Richman Owen	Circuit Judge	4	rejected, 53-42	no final vote
108th, 2003	Carolyn B. Kuhl	Circuit Judge	2	rejected, 53-43	no final vote
108th, 2003	Janice R. Brown	Circuit Judge	1	rejected, 53-43	no final vote
108th, 2003	Thomas C. Dorr	Undersecretary of Agriculture and Board Member, Commodity Credit Corporation[e]	2	rejected, 57-39	no final vote
108th, 2004	Marcia G. Cooke	District Judge	1	withdrawn	confirmed, 96-0
108th, 2004	William Gerry Myers III	Circuit Judge	1	rejected, 53-44	no final vote
108th, 2004	David W. McKeague	Circuit Judge	1	rejected, 53-44	no final vote

Table 6. (Continued)

Congress and Year	Nominee	Position	Number of Cloture Attempts[a]	Final Outcome of Cloture Attempt[b]	Disposition of Nominationc
108th, 2004	Henry W. Saad	Circuit Judge	1	rejected, 52-46	no final vote
108th, 2004	Richard A. Griffin	Circuit Judge	1	rejected, 54-44	no final vote
109th, 2005	Thomas C. Dorr	Undersecretary of Agriculture	1	withdrawn	confirmed, 62-38
109th, 2005	Priscilla Richman Owen	Circuit Judge	1	invoked, 81-18	confirmed, 55-43
109th, 2005	William H. Pryor, Jr.	Circuit Judge	1	invoked, 67-32	confirmed, 53-45
109th, 2005	Janice R. Brown	Circuit Judge	1	invoked, 65-32	confirmed, 56-43
109th, 2005	John R. Bolton	U.S. Representative to the United Nations	2	rejected, 54-38	no final vote
109th, 2005	Stephen L. Johnson	Administrator, Environmental Protection Agency	1	invoked, 61-37	confirmed, voice
109th, 2005	Robert J. Portman	U.S. Trade Representative	1	vitiated	confirmed, voice
109th, 2006	Peter Cyril Wyche Flory	Assistant Secretary of Defense	1	rejected, 52-41	no final vote
109th, 2006	Gordon England	Deputy Secretary of Defense	1	withdrawn	confirmed, voice
109th, 2006	Eric S. Edelman	Under Secretary of Defense	1	withdrawn	confirmed, voice
109th, 2006	Benjamin A. Powell	General Counsel, Office of the Director of National Intelligence	1	withdrawn	confirmed, voice
109th, 2006	Richard Stickler	Assistant Secretary of Labor	1	withdrawn	no final vote
109th, 2006	Dorrance Smith	Assistant Secretary of Defense	1	withdrawn	confirmed, 59-34
109th, 2006	Samuel A. Alito, Jr.	Associate Justice, Supreme Court	1	invoked, 72-25	confirmed, 58-42
109th, 2006	Brett M. Kavanaugh	Circuit Judge	1	invoked, 67-30	confirmed, 57-36
109th,	Andrew von	Commissioner, Food	1	invoked,	confirmed,

Congress and Year	Nominee	Position	Number of Cloture Attempts[a]	Final Outcome of Cloture Attempt[b]	Disposition of Nominationc
2006	Eschenbach	and Drug Administration		89-6	80-11
109th, 2006	Dirk Kempthorne	Secretary of the Interior	1	invoked, 85-8	confirmed, voice
109th, 2006	Kent A. Jordan	Circuit Judge	1	invoked, 93-0	confirmed, 91-0
110th, 2007	Leslie Southwick	Circuit Judge	1	invoked, 62-35	confirmed, 59-38
111th, 2009	Hilda Solis	Secretary of Labor	1	withdrawn	confirmed, 80-17
111th, 2009	Austan Dean Goolsbee	Member, Council of Economic Advisers	1	withdrawn	confirmed, UC
111th, 2009	Cecilia Elena Rouse	Member, Council of Economic Advisers	1	withdrawn	confirmed, UC
111th, 2009	David W. Ogden	Deputy Attorney General	1	withdrawn	confirmed, 65-28
111th, 2009	Christopher R. Hill	U.S. Ambassador to Iraq	1	invoked, 73-17	confirmed, 73-23
111th, 2009	Cass R. Sunstein	Administrator, Office of Information and Regulatory Affairs, Office of	1	invoked, 63-35	confirmed, 57-40
		Management and Budget			
111th, 2009	David J. Hayes	Deputy Secretary of the Interior	1	rejected, 57-39	confirmed, UC
111th, 2009	Robert M. Groves	Director of the Census, Department of Commerce	1	invoked, 76-15	confirmed, voice
111th, 2009	Harold Hongju Koh	Legal Advisor, Department of State	1	invoked, 65-31	confirmed, 62-35
111th, 2009	William K. Sessions III	Chair, United States Sentencing Commission	1	withdrawn	confirmed, UC
111th, 2009	David F. Hamilton	Circuit judge	1	invoked, 70-29	confirmed, 59-39
111th, 2010	Ben S. Bernanke	Chairman, Board of Governors, Federal Reserve System	1	invoked, 77-23	confirmed, 70-30

Table 6. (Continued)

Congress and Year	Nominee	Position	Number of Cloture Attempts[a]	Final Outcome of Cloture Attempt[b]	Disposition of Nominationc
111th, 2010	M. Patricia Smith	Solicitor, Department of Labor	1	invoked, 60-32	confirmed, 60-37
111th, 2010	Martha N. Johnson	Administrator, General Services Administration	1	invoked, 82-16	confirmed, 96-0
111th, 2010	Barbara Milano Keenan	Circuit Judge	1	invoked, 99-0	confirmed, 99-0
111th, 2010	Lael Brainard	Under Secretary, Treasury Department	1	invoked, 84-10	confirmed, 78-19
111th, 2010	Marisa J. Demeo	Associate Judge, Superior Court, District of Columbia	1	withdrawn	confirmed, 66-32
111th, 2010	Thomas J. Vanaskie	Circuit Judge	1	withdrawn	confirmed, 77-20
111th, 2010	Christopher H. Schroeder	Assistant Attorney General	1	withdrawn	confirmed, 72-24
111th, 2010	Denny Chin	Circuit Judge	1	withdrawn	confirmed, 98-0
111th, 2010	Craig Becker	Member, National Labor Relations Board	1	rejected, 52-33	no final vote
112th, 2011	Richard Cordray	Director, Bureau of Consumer Financial Protection	1	rejected, 53-45	no final vote
112th, 2011	Mari Carmen Aponte	Ambassador	2	invoked, 62-37	confirmed, voice
112th, 2011	Norman L. Eisen	Ambassador	1	invoked, 70-16	confirmed, voice
112th, 2011	Donald B. Verrilli	Solicitor General	1	withdrawn	confirmed, 72-16
112th, 2011	James Michael Cole	Deputy Attorney General	1	rejected, 50-40	confirmed, 55-42
112th, 2011	John J. McConnell, Jr.	District Judge	1	invoked, 63-33	confirmed, 50-44
112th, 2011	Caitlin Joan Halligan	Circuit Judge	1	rejected, 54-45	no final vote
112th, 2011	Goodwin Liu	Circuit Judge	1	rejected, 52-43	withdrawn
112th,	Jesse M.	District Judge	1	withdrawn	confirmed,

Congress and Year	Nominee	Position	Number of Cloture Attempts[a]	Final Outcome of Cloture Attempt[b]	Disposition of Nominationc
2012	Furman				62-34
112th, 2012	Adalberto Jose Jordan	Circuit Judge	1	invoked, 89-5	confirmed, 94-5
112th, 2012	Jerome H. Powell	Board of Governors, Federal Reserve System	1	withdrawn	confirmed, 74-21
112th, 2012	Jeremy C. Stein	Board of Governors, Federal Reserve System	1	withdrawn	confirmed, 70-24
112th, 2012	Michael A. Shipp	District Judge	1	withdrawn	confirmed, 91-1
112th, 2012	Robert E. Bacharach	Circuit Judge	1	rejected, 56-34	no final vote
112th, 2012	Timothy S. Hillman	District Judge	1	withdrawn	confirmed, 88-1
112th, 2012	John J. Tharp, Jr.	District Judge	1	withdrawn	confirmed, 86-1
112th, 2012	George Levi Russell, III	District Judge	1	withdrawn	confirmed, voice
112th, 2012	John Z. Lee	District Judge	1	withdrawn	confirmed, voice
112th, 2012	Kristine Gerhard Baker	District Judge	1	withdrawn	confirmed, voice
112th, 2012	Andrew David Hurwitz	Circuit Judge	1	invoked, 60-31	confirmed, voice
112th, 2012	Paul J. Watford	Circuit Judge	1	withdrawn	confirmed, 61-34
112th, 2012	Brian C. Wimes	District Judge	1	withdrawn	confirmed, 92-1
112th, 2012	David Campos Guaderrama	District Judge	1	withdrawn	confirmed, voice
112th, 2012	Gregg Jeffrey Costa	District Judge	1	withdrawn	confirmed, 97-2
112th, 2012	Gina Marie Groh	District Judge	1	withdrawn	confirmed, 95-2
112th, 2012	David Nuffer	District Judge	1	withdrawn	confirmed, 96-2
112th, 2012	Michael Walter Fitzgerald	District Judge	1	withdrawn	confirmed, 91-6

Table 6. (Continued)

Congress and Year	Nominee	Position	Number of Cloture Attempts[a]	Final Outcome of Cloture Attempt[b]	Disposition of Nominationc
112th, 2012	Ronnie Abrams	District Judge	1	withdrawn	confirmed, 96-2
112th, 2012	Rudolph Contreras	District Judge	1	withdrawn	confirmed, voice
112th, 2012	Miranda Du	District Judge	1	withdrawn	confirmed, 59-39
112th, 2012	Susie Morgan	District Judge	1	withdrawn	confirmed, 96-1
112th, 2012	Jeffrey J. Helmick	District Judge	1	withdrawn	confirmed, 62-36
112th, 2012	Mary Geiger Lewis	District Judge	1	withdrawn	confirmed, 64-29

Source: Compilations by CRS and Senate Library; Legislative Information System of the U.S. Congress; U.S. Congress, Senate, Committee on Rules and Administration, Senate Cloture Rule, committee print 99-95, 99th Congress, 1st session (Washington: GPO, 1985), pp. 44-70, 78-85; Congressional Record (Daily Digest); and Congressional Quarterly Almanac for 1986, 1987, 1992, 1995, 1999.

Notes: Executive branch nominations in roman; judicial nominations in italic. Final outcome of cloture attempt in bold when cloture was rejected. Disposition of nomination is in bold when nominee was not confirmed.

[a] Includes both cloture motions filed and votes of the Senate to reconsider a cloture vote.

[b] If more than one cloture vote occurred on a nomination, the tally displayed is that of the last such vote. The final outcome is given as "withdrawn," "vitiated," or "fell" only if no cloture vote occurred. "Withdrawn" and "vitiated" mean that the Senate disregarded the cloture motion and took no further action on it. "Fell" means that the cloture motion received no vote because it became moot.

[c] Vote tally, if roll call vote; "voice" if voice vote; "UC" if by unanimous consent.

[d] These five nominations to various positions in the State Department, which received consideration and cloture action concurrently, are counted as one case in this report.

[e] The individual was nominated concurrently for the two positions specified, and cloture action took place on each nomination in turn. For each nominee, the report counts the actions on both nominations as one case.

End Notes

[1] Filibusters and cloture are discussed more generally in CRS Report RL30360, Filibusters and Cloture in the Senate, by Richard S. Beth and Valerie Heitshusen. The process by which the Senate considers nominations is discussed more generally in CRS Report RL31980, Senate Consideration of Presidential Nominations: Committee and Floor Procedure, by Elizabeth Rybicki, and CRS Report RL31948, Evolution of the Senate's Role in the Nomination and Confirmation Process: A Brief History, by Betsy Palmer.

[2] Senate Rule XXII, paragraph 2, in U.S. Senate, Committee on Rules and Administration, Senate Manual, Containing the Standing Rules, Orders, Laws, and Resolutions Affecting the Business of the United States Senate, S.Doc. 112-1, 112th Cong., 2nd sess., prepared by Matthew McGowan under the direction of Jean Parvin Bordewich, staff director (Washington: GPO, 2011), sec. 22.2. During the 30 hours, no single Senator, other than the party floor leaders, the managers of the debate, or Senators to whom any of these may yield time, may occupy more than one hour in debate.

[3] This standing order was established by sec. 2 of S.Res. 15 of the 113th Congress, adopted January 25, 2013. For more detailed information on this standing order, see CRS Report R42996, Changes to Senate Procedures in the 113th Congress Affecting the Operation of Cloture (S.Res. 15 and S.Res. 16), by Elizabeth Rybicki.

[4] For further information on holds, see CRS Report 98-712, "Holds" in the Senate, and CRS Report RL31685, Proposals to Reform "Holds" in the Senate, both by Walter J. Oleszek.

[5] These questions of method are discussed in more detail in Richard S. Beth, "What We Don't Know About Filibusters," paper presented at the annual meeting of the Western Political Science Association, Portland, Ore., March 1995 (available from the author).

[6] U.S. Congress, Senate, Committee on Rules and Administration, Senate Cloture Rule: Limitation of Debate in the Congress of the United States and Legislative History of Paragraph 2 of Rule XXII of the Standing Rules of the United States Senate (Cloture Rule), S.Prt. 112-31, prepared by the Congressional Research Service, Library of Congress, 112th Cong., 1st sess. (Washington: GPO, 2011), pp. 17, 20-21, 185-192.

[7] For purposes of this report, five State Department nominations considered concurrently by unanimous consent are counted as one, and each instance in which a single individual was concurrently nominated to two positions is counted as one.

[8] The data include all cloture action in relation to a nomination, whether the motion was offered to close debate on the nomination itself or on a debatable motion to proceed to its consideration (which did not occur in practice after 1980).

[9] In the final case, on the nomination of Richard Stickler to be an Assistant Secretary of Labor in the 109th Congress (2006-2007), the cloture motion was withdrawn and the nomination was not confirmed.

[10] See G. Calvin Mackenzie, "Senatorial Courtesy," in Donald C. Bacon, Roger H. Davidson, and Morton Keller, eds., The Encyclopedia of the United States Congress, vol. 4 (New York: Simon & Schuster, (c)1995), pp. 1794-1795.

[11] Committee on Rules and Administration, Senate Cloture Rule, pp. 29-31, 60, 199-208.

[12] The five Congresses in question are the 103rd, 108th, 109th, 111th, and 112th. The Republican Party lost control of the Senate during the 1st session of the 107th Congress in 2001, at the beginning of the first term of President George W. Bush.

[13] For discussions of the possibilities for such proceedings, see CRS Report R42929, Procedures for Considering Changes in Senate Rules, and CRS Report RL32843, "Entrenchment" of

Senate Procedure and the "Nuclear Option" for Change: Possible Proceedings and Their Implications, both by Richard S. Beth.

[14] The three nominations were those of Don Zimmerman to be member of the National Labor Relations Board in 1980; William A. Lubbers to be its General Counsel in the same year; and Sam Brown, the former antiwar activist, to be Ambassador during his tenure as Head of Delegation to the Conference on Security and Cooperation in Europe in 1994. Only in the third case was cloture ultimately rejected and the nomination not confirmed.

[15] The two nominations were those of John R. Bolton to be U.S. Representative to the United Nations in 2005 and Mari Carmen Aponte to be Ambassador to El Salvador in 2011. Only in the first case was cloture ultimately rejected and the nomination not confirmed.

[16] The two nominations were, respectively, those of Miguel A. Estrada and Pricilla Richman Owen to be Circuit Court Judges. In both cases, cloture was ultimately rejected and the nomination not confirmed.

[17] This point is discussed, for example, in Michael J. Gerhardt, The Federal Appointments Process: A Constitutional and Historical Analysis (Durham: Duke University Press, 2003), pp. 132-133.

INDEX

A

B

C

D

E

F

G

H

I

J

L

M

N

O

P

Q

R

S

T

U

V

W